NEW JERSEY ASK5

LANGUAGE ARTS LITERACY TEST

Mark Riccardi and Kimberly Perillo, M.Ed.

BARRON'S

About the Authors

Mark Riccardi has been a Language Arts teacher in a middle school in South Brunswick, New Jersey, for the past ten years. He received his BA in English Education from Trenton State College. He lives with his wife, April, and two sons, Connor and Cameron, in Ocean County.

Kimberly Perillo is a middle school reading specialist in South Brunswick, New Jersey. She is a graduate of Trenton State College, now TCNJ, and has a Master's degree in Reading from Rutgers University. She has been a teacher trainer in reading strategies since 2005 and loves helping children understand challenging texts. She lives with her husband, John, and two children, Abigail and Robert, in Mercer County.

All inquiries should be addressed to:
Barron's Educational Series, Inc.
250 Wireless Boulevard
Hauppauge, NY 11788
www.barronseduc.com

ISBN-13: 978-0-7641-4294-9
ISBN-10: 0-7641-4294-1

Library of Congress Catalog Card No.: 2009008054

Library of Congress Cataloging-in-Publication Data:

Perillo, Kimberly.
  New Jersey ASK5 Language Arts Literacy Test / Kimberly Perillo and Mark Riccardi.
      p. cm.
  Includes index.
  ISBN-13: 978-0-7641-4294-9
  ISBN-10: 0-7641-4294-1
  1. Language arts (Elementary)–New Jersey–Examinations–Study guides.
  2. New Jersey Assessment of Skills and Knowledge–Study guides.   I. Riccardi, Mark   II. Title.   III. Title: New Jersey ASK Five Language Arts Literacy Test.

LB1576.P535 2009
372.6076–dc22

2009008054

Date of Manufacture: January 2013
Manufactured by: B11R11, Robbinsville, NJ

10%
POST-CONSUMER
WASTE
Paper contains a minimum of 10% post-consumer waste (PCW). Paper used in this book was derived from certified, sustainable forestlands.

Printed in the United States of America
9 8 7 6 5 4

CONTENTS

Important Note: Barron's has made every effort to ensure the content of this book is accurate as of press time, but New Jersey state exams are constantly changing. Be sure to consult **www.state.nj.us/education/assessment** for all the latest New Jersey state testing information. Regardless of the changes that may be announced after press time, this book will still provide a very strong framework for fifth-grade students preparing for the exam.

INTRODUCTION— MEET THE TEST

Congratulations! You are on your way to achieving your best possible score on the NJ ASK Language Arts and Literacy test for Grade 5. By using all of the lessons, hints, and tips in this book, you should be able to earn your best score. Before we begin, read through the information on the next few pages. Hopefully this information will answer any questions you might have about the test.

What Is the NJ ASK LAL?

The NJ ASK is the New Jersey Assessment of Skills and Knowledge. This test is given to every public school student in New Jersey in grades three through eight. Every year, students are tested in Language Arts and Literacy (LAL) and Math. In fourth and eighth grade, students are tested in Science as well. The focus of this book will be on the Language Arts and Literacy section for fifth grade students.

Why Do I Need to Take This Test?

Every public school student in the state of New Jersey takes this test. The state can then see that every student is able to complete tasks that are equal to his or her grade level. Schools can use the results of the test to make sure their students are receiving the right programs and help any students who are struggling.

How Will This Book Help?

This book will help you prepare to take every part of the NJ ASK LAL Grade 5 test. You should be well prepared for this test if you attend school every day and try your best. The test is meant to test what every fifth grade student should know. This book gives you tips and techniques that we know will give you an advantage when you take the test. The book will set up real test situations so that when you take the real test, you will be used to the way the test looks. The more practice you have, the better you will do.

What Will This Book Cover?

The test is split into four parts: a persuasive essay, a speculative **or** explanatory essay, an everyday text reading passage with questions, and a narrative text reading passage with questions. There are both multiple-choice and open-ended questions. This book will explain each of these parts.

What Kind of Writing Will I Do?

On the NJ ASK5, you will need to complete two writing tasks. In this book, we will show you how to write a persuasive, speculative, and explanatory prompt. You will only need to do two types, but you will be prepared to do any of the three that are included on the test.

What Else Can I Do to Get Ready?

After using the tips and techniques in this book, the rest is up to you. The best way to prepare for this test is to do your best everyday. Pay attention in school, do all of your work, and do your best. During the week of the test, make sure you get plenty of rest every night, eat a good breakfast, and bring a positive attitude. With a lot of preparation and the right attitude, you can accomplish anything.

If I Complete This Book, Will I Be Guaranteed to Pass the Test?

Unfortunately, we cannot guarantee that you will pass the test if you do the work in this book. The book will put you in the best possible position for success. If any section is difficult for you, make sure you go back over it again and take notes. Ask a parent or teacher to help you check work that you find difficult. Work hard and do your best. That is all you can ask of yourself. Now let's get going and prepare for the NJ ASK!

PERSUASIVE WRITING

WHAT IS PERSUASIVE WRITING?

One of the types of writing that you will have to complete on the NJ ASK5 is the Persuasive Writing task. Even if you do not have experience writing persuasive essays, you do not need to worry. It is likely that you are doing some type of persuading every day. Have you ever tried to convince a parent to buy something for you? Talked your friends into playing the game you want to play? Tried to convince a brother or sister to let you watch a show on television? All of these require you to persuade, or convince, the person you are speaking to that your opinion is the best one. On the NJ ASK5 you will be given a writing prompt or task to complete. You will then plan, write, and edit an essay. Do not worry if this task sounds difficult. If you follow and practice the steps in this chapter, you will have no problem completing the task to the best of your ability.

This chapter will break the essay into its most basic parts: choosing a side, prewriting, and writing the essay itself including the introduction, body, and conclusion. Once you have mastered each part, you will have the opportunity to put it all together. Ready? Let's get started!

BEGIN AT THE BEGINNING

It can be said that your score on the Persuasive Writing task could be decided in the first 5 minutes of the test. Does this sound crazy? It might, but your first two choices could decide how well you do on this part of the test. The first part will be to read the prompt in the test booklet. Remember, you can write in the test booklet. As you read the prompt, underline the part of the prompt that asks you the question. The prompt will contain all of the background information you will need to begin writing, but they will only ask you one question. Make sure you know what is being asked of you. Read the following prompt and answer the question that follows.

> Your school can take one field trip at the end of the school year. Your teachers and principal would like to know what the students think about possible places to visit. They are asking each student to write a letter to the principal explaining his or her choice for a field trip.
>
> Write a letter to your principal explaining your choice of field trip. Be sure to give reasons to support your choice in a well-planned, effective letter. You may choose to prewrite before beginning your letter.

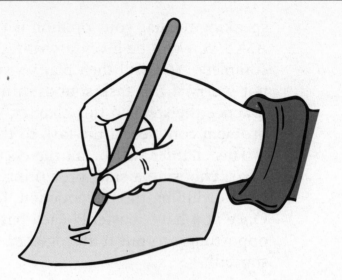

PRACTICE

Which of the following statements from the prompt includes your task? Circle your answer.

    A. Your teachers and principal would like to know what the students think about possible places to visit.

    B. Be sure to give reasons to support your choice in a well-planned, effective letter.

    C. Write a letter to your principal explaining your choice of field trip.

The question you are being asked could be tricky. Why? This is because you are not being asked a specific question. You are being given a task. Therefore the correct answer is C. Let's go through each of the three choices.

■ A is incorrect because the sentence is giving you background information about the problem. You need this information, but it does not tell you what to do.

■ B is incorrect because the sentence gives you advice for the task itself. It lets you know that you should support your choice, but it does not tell you what to do.

- ▪ C is the correct choice because it gives you the task. This is the prompt. It is the part that tells you what to do. What are you supposed to do? Write a letter to your principal explaining your choice of field trip.

So you now know that you have to write a letter picking a field trip location. We know what our essay is about. Let's move on to the next step.

PICKING A SIDE OR MAKING A CHOICE

Now that you know what your task is, you can concentrate on the second major choice you have—deciding what to write about. The Persuasive Writing task will ask you to choose either a side of a problem or a solution to a problem. Each of them has a different way to help you make a decision. Let's start with choosing a solution.

Here is our prompt again.

> Your school can take one field trip at the end of the school year. Your teachers and principal would like to know what the students think about possible places to visit. They are asking each student to write a letter to the principal explaining his or her choice for a field trip.
>
> Write a letter to your principal explaining your choice of field trip. Be sure to give reasons to support your choice in a well-planned, effective letter. You may choose to prewrite before beginning your letter.

We know that we are writing a letter to the principal. What are we going to write about? Answer the following questions to help you make your decision. Try to answer them quickly as if you were taking the real test.

1. What fun and/or educational places are within two hours of your school? Try to come up with two or three places.

   _____

   _____

   _____

2. Which of your choices would give the most students a chance to have fun and learn something?

   _____

3. What place do you think is the most affordable?

   _____

4. Look at your answers. What is your choice?

   _____

   _____

   _____

Excellent job! When you are taking the test, you will need to ask yourself questions like these to help you make a choice. Remember, you have to think quickly so you have plenty of time to write. By practicing in this book, you will improve that ability.

Now we have to look at the other type of persuasive essay that may be given to you—picking a side. You will be asked to choose one side of a problem and explain why it is the better choice. Read the prompt below and answer the questions that follow.

> Recently, students in the cafeteria have not been listening to directions. They have been leaving behind garbage, not pushing in chairs, and not listening to the adults in the cafeteria. Your principal has decided that every lunch will be silent. This decision has caused a controversy in your school.
>
> Write a letter to your principal stating your opinion about the decision. Use specific examples and reasons to support your opinion.

PRACTICE

1. What is the task you are being asked to do? Remember to look for the one sentence that will give you the task.

   _____

   _____

   _____

2. What are the two opinions you could have?

   _____

   _____

   _____

3. Which of these choices do you agree with?

_____

_____

_____

Now that you have answered these questions, let's look at the possible answers.

Answers

1. The task you are being asked to do is to write a letter to your principal stating your opinion about the decision. Remember you are looking for your task or writing assignment.

2. Your principal has made a decision. You have two choices. You can either agree with the decision or disagree with the decision.

3. You can choose either side you want. It is your essay. You can support the principal's decision or oppose the principal's decision. Just remember, this story is fictional or made up. You can pick the side that you think is easier to write about.

If you are having trouble choosing a side, you can make a quick chart to see which side is easier. This is called deciding the pros and cons. Pros are the positives, and cons are the negatives. Look at the chart below. It has been filled out for you already.

PRO	CON
Students will learn to respect adults.	Students will not have chance to talk to friends.
Students will concentrate on better behavior.	Silence will not get students to clean up their mess.
Students will clean up quicker.	Silence will affect behavior in other places.

We have three choices for each side. Each of these could be a reason in our essay. Which one do you think would be easier to write about? Good. Now that you know how to quickly choose your opinion, let's move on to the second major step of our essay writing: prewriting.

PREWRITING

How well you prewrite could very well make the difference between a passing and failing score on this part of the NJ ASK. This seems strange since the prewriting is not graded. Prewriting is important because the better you plan, the easier time you will have writing. It is written in the test that you may want to spend 5 to 10 minutes planning your ideas. By using that time, you will actually use less time writing. We will go through each step and give you opportunities to practice. The more you practice prewriting, the easier it will be when you take the test.

After you made your choice, you can now plan the essay. This is done by prewriting. Prewriting is the place to organize your thoughts so you have an easy time writing the essay. The best way to organize your thoughts is by using a graphic organizer. A graphic organizer is a picture or chart that helps you split the essay into different parts to help you keep all of your thoughts in order. Since there are five parts to the persuasive essay—introduction, three body paragraphs, and the conclusion—we need a graphic organizer that has five parts. We like to create a drawing that is easy to draw and easy to split into five parts. Using the drawing, it makes it easier to remember the different parts of the essay, in case you forget. The drawing we are going to use in this book is a piece of cake because we think that, if you follow and practice all of the advice in this book, the NJ ASK5 will be a piece of cake! Now let's look at our piece of cake and what each part represents.

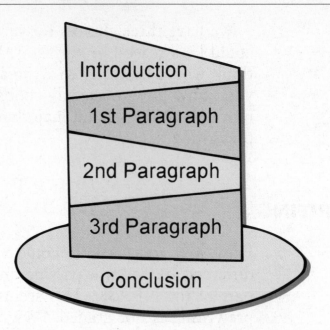

See? A piece of cake. How do you fill it in? You have to go step by step and fill in each part so you are ready to write your essay. Let's go back to the writing prompt and remember what your choice is. Here is the prompt again.

> Your school can take one field trip at the end of the school year. Your teachers and principal would like to know what the students think about possible places to visit. They are asking each student to write a letter to the principal explaining his or her choice for a field trip.
>
> Write a letter to your principal explaining your choice of field trip. Be sure to give reasons to support your choice in a well-planned, effective letter. You may choose to prewrite before beginning your letter.

What was your choice for a field trip? Write it here.

_____

_____

To show you how to fill in the graphic organizer, we chose a state park in New Jersey, Island Beach State Park.

We will use this to create the graphic organizer. Since we have already chosen the place, let's begin. First the introduction.

INTRODUCTION

The introduction is the frosting. It is tasty, people usually look forward to it, and they can get a good idea if the rest of the cake is going to be good. The introduction is very important and has three parts. They are the interest catcher, thesis statement, and three reasons. The interest catcher will be the first part of your essay, but the thesis statement is the most important, so we will start with that part first. Each part is explained below.

THESIS STATEMENT

The thesis statement is the one sentence that will tell the reader what your essay is about. If every other sentence is eliminated from the essay, the thesis statement will tell the reader what you think, feel, and believe.

For this essay, we are choosing a place to go for a field trip. Your thesis should be a simple statement that tells the reader exactly where you want to go. When you write your sentence, try not to use the word "I." Here is our example.

> The field trip that our school should choose is Island Beach State Park.

Now write your thesis below:

_____

_____

_____

Excellent work!

SUPPORTING REASONS

The next part of our introduction is the three supporting reasons that you will use to support your thesis. They should be clear and be directly related to your thesis. You just wrote your thesis, so read it again. What can you do to prove to the reader that your idea is the best one for your school? Let's look below at our example thesis and see what reasons can support it.

Example thesis: The field trip that our school should choose is Island Beach State Park.

Reason #1: Island Beach State Park has educational opportunities.

Reason #2: This is an opportunity for students to go somewhere new.

Reason #3: While the trip is educational, students will also have fun.

Now it is your turn to create your three supporting reasons. Rewrite your thesis on the lines below and then write your three reasons in the space provided.

Your thesis:

_____

_____

Remember each of your reasons must support your thesis. They should be clear but do not need to be too specific. You will have that opportunity in the body of the essay.

Reason #1:

_____

_____

Reason #2:

_____

_____

Reason #3:

_____

_____

Do all of your reasons support the thesis? Are all of them about the place you chose for the trip? If one or more do not support your thesis, change them now. When you are ready, move on to the final part of your introduction.

INTEREST CATCHER

The first part of your opening paragraph should give the reader an idea about your essay, but not tell them everything. It should make them want to read more. It can be more than one sentence, but it should not take you too long to write. There are a few different types of interest catchers you could use. They are the rhetorical question, startling fact, and descriptive scene. Let's look at each one. Then you can practice creating an interest catcher for each one.

Rhetorical Question

A rhetorical question is a question that does not require an answer. They are meant to get someone's attention or encourage them to think about a topic. An example of a rhetorical question could be "Why does this always happen to me?" or "Can you believe they are closing the movie theater?" For our essay it could be "Did you know that most students in our school have never seen the ocean?" The person who is asking the question doesn't need you to answer. They just want you to think about the topic or what is happening.

Startling Fact

Nothing gets someone's attention faster than a shocking fact or idea. If it is something that they never thought about before, they will be interested in knowing more. You can use math and create a number that will get someone's attention. "Eighty-seven percent of fifth graders at our school have never been to the ocean." It should be something that will cause the reader to say, "I can't believe that." A startling fact could be "More students failed the test than passed." That would get your attention. You would worry that you were one of the people who failed.

Descriptive Scene

A descriptive scene is the most difficult of the three types of interest catchers. It means exactly what it says. You start the essay with a short description of a scene. If you do it right, the reader will have a picture in his or her head that will give you the opportunity to get your point across. A descriptive scene could be more than one sentence. Here is an example:

> Imagine students at the edge of the ocean collecting water in buckets so they can check for jellyfish. The surf crashes and boys and girls are sent scattering like hermit crabs along the sand. Another group of students are following a guide along the dunes, examining the grass and looking for areas that storms have damaged.

Do you have a picture in your head of what the students are doing at the beach? They are having fun, doing work, and exploring the beach area. These are all things you can see, and it gives you the opportunity to convince the reader that going to the beach on a field trip is the best idea. Are you ready to try some on your own? Great! If you need to look back to check on your topic, you should do that now.

PRACTICE

Rhetorical question:

_____

_____

Startling fact:

_____

_____

_____

_____

Descriptive scene (don't write more that two or three sentences):

_____

_____

_____

_____

_____

Your answers will vary by the topic you chose, but you can ask yourself questions to see if you are on the right track. Do I ask a question that the reader has to think about before answering? Will the reader most likely agree with me? Will my fact shock others? Does my scene have enough description to put a picture in the reader's head?

Excellent job. This may seem like a lot, especially since this part of the prewriting is only for the introduction, but if you work hard on these parts, writing the essay is going to be a piece of cake!

BODY PARAGRAPHS AND SUPPORTING DETAILS

Right now, you might be asking yourself, "Why do I have to prewrite for the supporting paragraphs if I already have my three reasons?" The answer is that this is where most students lose points on the NJ ASK. The writer has three good reasons but has not written anything to support them. Because of this, the writer receives a lower score than expected. For the prewriting part of this essay, we are going to concentrate on how you can support your reasons with persuasive techniques. Persuasive techniques are tools you can use to help you be more convincing. You will even be able to use them when having a discussion with someone to better prove your point. We are going to learn to use four persuasive techniques. They are bandwagon, scientific data, expert opinion, and positive/negative consequences.

The three layers of cake are your supporting paragraphs. These are the important parts that are the substance of your essay. Without these paragraphs, your readers will not know why they should believe your side or opinion. To support your three reasons you need details, specific details. Persuasive techniques are ways for you to support your reasons in a way that will convince your readers to believe in your opinion. Each of the four techniques will be explained and there will be an opportunity to practice each type following the explanation.

BANDWAGON

"But Mom, everyone has a cell phone. If I don't have one, I'll be the only one." Does this argument sound familiar? What this person is doing is using a persuasive technique called bandwagon. The bandwagon technique is an argument that shows that most or all of a group of people are participating in an activity or believe in the same thing. It is the most simple way of persuading. It can be very convincing. By showing that almost everyone believes something, it suggests that the reader should believe it too. Let's try it out. We have listed one of our

reasons below with a sentence supporting it using bandwagon. After reading the sentence, see if you can create a bandwagon sentence using one of your reasons.

Reason #1: Island Beach State Park has educational opportunities.

Bandwagon sentence: Since most of the students in our school have never been to Island Beach State Park, everyone thinks it would be a great place to visit and learn something new.

Now it is your turn. Write your reason below and then write your supporting detail using bandwagon.

Reason #1:

_____

_____

Bandwagon sentence:

_____

_____

_____

_____

Great job! Does your bandwagon sentence make it sound like everyone wants to go visit your place? Excellent! Let's look at our second persuasive technique.

SCIENTIFIC DATA

Scientific data is a fancy way of saying numbers. You use the numbers and percentages to prove your point in a persuasive essay. Nine out of ten people prefer summer instead of winter. Eighty-five percent of fifth grade students would like to have physical education five times a week. The trick with using scientific data is that it has to sound believable. You do not have time to do any research, so the numbers you use will be made up. You are showing the people who score your test that you know how to use different persuasive techniques. Let's use scientific data to prove one of our reasons. Read the example below and then create your own.

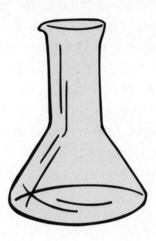

Reason #2: This is an opportunity for students to go somewhere new.

Scientific data sentence: In a survey of students in my class, 84 percent of the students want to go to Island Beach State Park.

Now it is your turn. Write your reason below and then write your supporting detail using scientific data.

Reason #2:

_____

_____

Scientific data sentence:

_____

_____

_____

_____

Excellent! Does your scientific data sentence use a number that helps prove your point? Fantastic! Let's look at our third persuasive technique.

EXPERT OPINION

If you have trouble with a math problem, whom do you ask? Your math teacher, right? That is because your math teacher is the expert. If you have a bad cold, you would go to the doctor because he or she is the expert that helps you stay healthy. So in a persuasive essay, you would use an use an expert to help prove your side of the issue. Again, remember that you will be creating the expert, so make sure that it is believable. Read the example below and then try out your own.

Reason #3: While the trip is educational, students will also have fun.

Expert opinion sentence: A leading expert of 10- and 11-year-old children wrote that when students are having fun, they learn more.

Now it is your turn. Write your reason below and then write your supporting detail using expert opinion.

Reason #3:

_____

_____

Expert opinion sentence:

_____

_____

_____

_____

Excellent! Does your expert opinion sentence use a person that helps prove your point? Fantastic! Let's look at our final persuasive technique.

Positive and Negative Consequences

Positive consequences means that, when you do something, good things will happen. Negative consequences means that the result of your actions will cause something bad. You can choose one or the other for your essay. We have an example below for both positive and negative consequences. Read the examples and then choose one to try on your sentence. We will use reason #3 again.

Reason #3: Even though the trip is educational, students will also have fun.

Positive consequence sentence: If our class has the chance to go to Island Beach State Park, many students will learn about ways to keep the ocean clean and be friendlier to the environment.

Negative consequence sentence: If our class does not go to Island Beach State Park, many students will not understand why it is important to have clean oceans.

Now it is your turn. Choose positive or negative consequences and write a sentence supporting your reason.

Reason #3:

_____

_____

Positive/negative consequence sentence:

_____

_____

_____

_____

Does your positive/negative consequence sentence show what will happen if your opinion is chosen? Great! We are done prewriting our body paragraphs. We only have one part left, the conclusion.

CONCLUSION

The conclusion is not part of the piece of cake. It is the plate, supporting all of the reasons and explanations you have written so far. Without a solid plate, the whole cake would fall down. The conclusion has three parts to it, and two of them are very easy to do. The three parts of the conclusion are restating the thesis, restating the three reasons, and a call to action.

When you are restating your thesis and reasons, you want to remind your readers what your opinion is, but you do not want to write it exactly the same way. Since we are prewriting now, you do not need to worry about restating them in your graphic organizer, but you do need to make sure they are written in the conclusion of your essay. The part of the conclusion that you do need to think about when you are prewriting is your final statement. This is called your call to action sentence. It is a sentence that asks your readers to make a decision or do something based on what you have written in your essay. So in our example essay, we want to tell the principal that he needs to choose our destination for the class trip. Read the example below and then take a turn writing your own call to action.

> **Call to action:** For the students of our school to have an experience they will never forget, the only choice is Island Beach State Park.

Now it is your turn. Try to write your call to action statement below.

Call to action:

_____

_____

_____

_____

Well Done! Is your call to action statement specific? Does it tell your readers exactly what you want them to do? Great. Now we are done with our prewriting lessons. Remember, the idea is that you will plan these ideas quickly and then move on to the essay. Here is what the prewriting for the example essay would look like.

Interest catcher:	Descriptive Scene—students learning and having fun at the beach.
Thesis statement:	The field trip that our school should choose is Island Beach State Park.
Three reasons: #1	—Island Beach State Park has educational opportunities.
#2	—This is an opportunity for students to go somewhere new.
#3	—Even though the trip is educational, students will also have fun.
Body paragraph one:	Persuasive technique used: Bandwagon
Body paragraph two:	Persuasive technique used: Scientific data
Body paragraph three:	Persuasive technique used: Expert opinion
Conclusion:	Restate thesis, restate three reasons, call to action—convince principal to choose Island Beach State Park as a trip.

What do you notice about this table? Did you notice that everything is not written out completely? This is because the prewriting is the time for you to think about the essay and write down ideas about what the essay will include. You will add the details when you write the essay.

PRACTICE

Now it is your turn to write the prewriting for your essay. On the next page is a blank graphic organizer. This organizer has a reminder about what you should write in each part. When you write the practice essay, you will be given a blank graphic organizer. As you fill in the graphic organizer, make sure you pay attention to each part. Try to complete it quickly, but do not forget to complete everything. The prompt is written below to remind you.

> Your school can take one field trip at the end of the school year. Your teachers and principal would like to know what the students think about possible places to visit. They are asking each student to write a letter to the principal explaining his or her choice for a field trip.
>
> Write a letter to your principal explaining your choice of field trip. Be sure to give reasons to support your choice in a well-planned, effective letter. You may choose to prewrite before beginning your letter.

GRAPHIC ORGANIZER

Interest catcher: Remember to write what type of interest catcher.

_____
_____
_____
_____

Thesis statement:

_____
_____

Three reasons:
#1—

_____
_____

#2—

_____
_____

#3—

_____
_____

Body paragraph one: Persuasive technique used:

_____
_____
_____
_____

Body paragraph two: Persuasive technique used:

_____
_____
_____
_____

Body paragraph three: Persuasive technique used:

_____
_____
_____
_____

Conclusion: Restate thesis, restate three reasons, call to action

_____
_____
_____
_____
_____

How did you do? Read over your table again. It is time to write the essay. On the next four pages, write your essay. Good luck. Make sure you only take 45 minutes to write the essay. Have someone time you or set a timer so you know how much time you have left. Make sure you leave time to edit and revise your work.

Here is an example of a persuasive essay that would receive a high score on the NJ ASK5. Read the essay and think about the essay you wrote. Do you notice anything you are missing or would change?

Imagine students at the edge of the ocean collecting water in buckets so they can check for jellyfish. The surf crashes and boys and girls are sent scattering like hermit crabs along the sand. Another group of students is following a guide along the dunes, examining the grass and looking for areas that storms have damaged. Fifth grade students have been asked to suggest places to go on an end of the year field trip. The field trip that our school should choose is Island Beach State Park. This is because Island Beach State Park has educational opportunities, it is an opportunity for students to go somewhere new, and even though the trip is educational, students will also have fun.

First of all, Island Beach State Park has educational opportunities. It would be nice to go to the beach and swim or lay in the sun, but the park has many things to teach kids our age. The ocean has different kinds of animals, the grass dunes protect the sand, and many things are hidden beneath the sand. In a survey of the 84 students in fifth grade, all of them think that going to Island Beach State Park is a good idea. This shows that no one will be disappointed. Educational opportunities are not the only reason Island Beach State Park is a good idea.

Next, this is an opportunity for students to go somewhere new. Did you know that 86 percent of the fifth grade students in our school have never been to Island Beach State Park? That is a very high number. We are obviously missing out on a great opportunity. It is important that all students have a chance to see how great this park is.

Finally, not only will students learn something, they will also have fun. My cousin went on a trip to Island Beach State Park with her class. She said that it was the best trip she has ever been on. A leading expert of 10- and 11-year-old children wrote that when students are having fun, they learn more. This is important because the more fun kids have, the more we want to learn.

In conclusion, the trip that our school should take is to Island Beach State Park. This is because Island Beach State Park has educational opportunities, it is an opportunity for students to go somewhere new, and even though the trip is educational, students will also have fun. It is the chance of a lifetime for all of the students. For the students of our school to have an experience they will never forget, the only choice is Island Beach State Park.

Hints for Success

If you follow all of the parts of essay writing included in this chapter, you should do well on this part of the NJ ASK5. There are, however, a few more things that you can do to push your score to the highest level possible. Study each part and then take the quiz that follows.

TRANSITIONS

Transitions are the bridges between paragraphs and sentences in your essay. They are the words that let your readers know that you are moving on to a new idea or explaining an old idea. There are two types of transitions, internal and external. Internal transitions are used in the middle of a paragraph to connect two sentences. External transitions are used to begin paragraphs so the reader knows a new idea is being started. Here are some examples of each.

Internal Transitions			
For example	Because of this	Therefore	However
Then	Immediately	Next	At this point

External Transitions			
First of all	Second	Most importantly	Finally
In conclusion	Next		

Word Choice

Using strong words helps your writing be clearer and more enjoyable for your readers. A great writer can pick the perfect word at the right place. Remember to use the best vocabulary you can when writing your essay. Do not write "good" when you can write "fantastic." Avoid "bad" when you can use "horrible." Your readers will have a better understanding of your essay, and your sophisticated vocabulary will help increase your score. Be careful. It is okay if you misspell a word here or there, but make sure that if you use difficult vocabulary, you know how to spell the word. If you write "horrible," but spell it "horible," that is not too bad. If you spell it "haribel," however, the reader may not understand what word you mean. The NJ ASK5 is a chance for you to show how much you know, so be awesome, stupendous, and excellent, not just good.

SENTENCE STRUCTURE

In the last chapter of this book, there are lessons and examples about grammar. Make sure you do all of the work in that chapter so you do not make simple mistakes. One part of that chapter that is worth repeating here is sentence structure. Writing complete sentences helps your readers understand what you are writing about. If your readers must stop and reread sentences because they do not make sense or are too long, your essay will receive a lower score. Make sure every sentence is complete and makes sense.

PRACTICE

Hints for Success

Are you ready for a quiz? Circle the correct answer on each multiple-choice question and then check your answers when you are done.

1. An appropriate transition to use when starting the paragraph after the introduction is _____.

   A. finally

   B. for example

   C. first of all

   D. however

2. A better way to write the word "funny" is _____.

   A. hysterical

   B. horrible

   C. depressing

   D. cute

3. Which of the following sentences is a complete sentence?

   A. I ran quickly to the store down the street from my house.

   B. Ran quickly down the street.

   C. I walked.

   D. Both A and C

4. Which transition would be used to start a sentence using a persuasive technique?

   A. For example

   B. First of all

   C. In conclusion

   D. Next

5. Fill in the blank with the best word. I felt _____ after taking my math test.

   A. horrible

   B. bad

   C. worse

   D. lonely

6. Which sentence below is *not* a complete sentence?

   A. I took a test.

   B. I ran a mile, but it took a long time.

   C. I fell off my chair when he told me the joke.

   D. I slipped on the ice, I bruised my knee, I bumped my head.

   (Answers on pp. 157–158.)

PRACTICE WRITING

It is time to write an essay from beginning to end. Read the prompt below, underline the important parts, pick a side, prewrite, and write your essay. Ask someone to set a timer for you or let you know when 45 minutes have passed. This will give you an idea how you are managing your time. The more you practice using the appropriate time, the better you will get at finishing in 45 minutes. A blank piece of cake prewriting template has been given to you, but none of the information has been filled in. You also have four pages to write your essay. An example essay and explanation can be found at the end of chapter. Good Luck.

> Your town is in the process of deciding what activities and sports they should offer for children your age. The mayor is looking for ideas. He has asked that children write a letter telling him what their favorite after school activity is and why your town should offer it to children. Remember, it should be something that many children could participate in.
>
> Write a letter explaining your favorite activity and why it should be a part of your town's after-school activity program.

GRAPHIC ORGANIZER

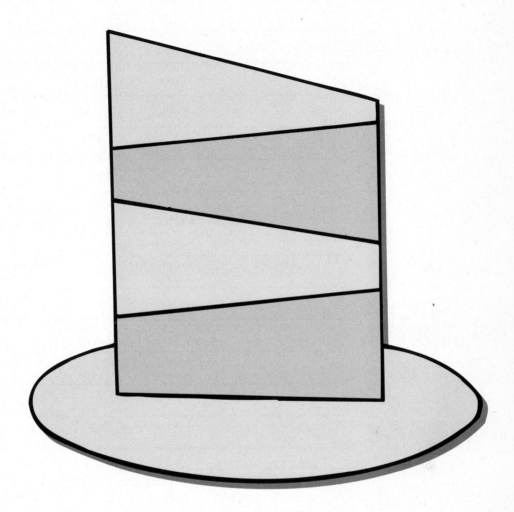

How did you do? Read over your table again. It is time to write the essay. On the next four pages, write your essay. Good luck. Make sure you only take 45 minutes to write the essay. Have someone time you or set a timer so you know how much time you have left. Make sure you leave time to edit and revise your work.

(Answers on pp. 158–160.)

New Jersey Holistic Rubric

Language Arts Literacy				
Writing				
New Jersey Holistic Scoring Rubric – Grade 5				
In scoring, consider the grid of written language	Inadequate Command	Limited Command	Partial Command	Adequate Command	Strong Command
Score	**1**	**2**	**3**	**4**	**5**
Content & Organization	May lack opening and/or closing	May lack opening and/or closing	May lack opening and/or closing	Generally has opening and/or closing	Opening and closing
	Minimal response to topic; uncertain focus	Attempts to focus	Usually has single focus	Single focus	Single focus
		May drift or focus			Sense of unity and coherence
					Key ideas developed
	No planning evident; Disorganized	Attempts organization	Some lapses or flaws in organization	Ideas loosely connected	Logical progression of ideas
		Few, if any, transitions between ideas	May lack some transitions between ideas	Transition evident	Moderately fluent
					Attempts compositional risks
	Details random, inappropriate, or barely apparent	Details lack elaboration that could highlight paper	Repetitive details	Uneven development details	Details appropriate and varied
			Several unelaborated details		
Usage	No apparent control	Numerous	Errors/patterns of errors may be evident	Some errors do not interfere with meaning	Few errors
	Severe/numerous errors				
Sentence Construction	Assortment of incomplete and/ or incorrect sentences	Excessive monotony/same structure	Little variety in syntax	Some variety	Variety in syntax appropriate and effective
		Numerous errors	Some errors	Generally correct	
Mechanics	Errors so severe they detract from meaning	Numerous serious errors	Patterns of errors evident	No consistent pattern of errors	Few errors
				Some errors that do not interfere with meaning	

Chapter 2

READING NARRATIVE TEXT

WHAT IS NARRATIVE TEXT?

YOU will face two types of reading on the NJ ASK5. The first type is called narrative text. You do not need to worry because you already know about narrative text. Narrative simply means a story, so on this part of the test, you will read a short story and answer questions. Some of the questions will be multiple-choice, and one will be open-ended. In multiple-choice questions, you have options, and you will need to choose the best answer. For the open-ended question, you will need to write a paragraph and use evidence from the text to support your opinion. In this chapter, you will learn strategies for reading and answering every type of question on the NJ ASK5.

READING FOR UNDERSTANDING

As you read the narrative story, it is really important that you use strategies to help you understand and remember the text as you read. You will have 30 minutes for this part of the test, and you don't want to waste time rereading. Your goal is to read and understand the first time! Now, you might be tempted to look ahead and read the questions first, but you should not do this! You might be asking, "Why not?" Perhaps you've even had someone tell you this is a good strategy to use. If you read the questions ahead of time, you probably will not focus on all of the details of the story, and guess what? You will need ALL of the details of the story to answer the open-ended question well.

Now, how can you accomplish this goal? You are going to apply reading strategies and interact with the text. This may slow your reading slightly, but it will be well worth it if you don't have to go back later and reread for every question on the test. Take a few minutes to review the reading strategies below.

Reading Strategies

- Predict—Guess what will happen in the story.
- Question—Ask questions of the author and text.
- Connect—Make connections between the story and your life, other text, or the world.
- Summarize—Stop periodically and retell what has happened so far in the story.
- Visualize—Picture what is happening in your head.
- Context clues—If you don't know a word, use the words around it to try and figure it out.

Let's give it a try. We're going to read two paragraphs from a story and try to interact with the text. You will see my thoughts in parentheses. Afterwards, you will have a chance to practice! You will need to slow down your reading to do this, but you will have an easier time remembering the story later!

The Look

As I walked through the front door, I saw my mom standing in the foyer, her arms crossed, and the look I knew all too well on her face. *(I think this mom is angry. I wonder what happened?)* It was the look that most mom's mastered early on in your childhood, the look that let you know to knock it off or else. *(I remember getting the look from my mom when I was arguing with my sister at a restaurant.)* The worst-case scenario was walking through the front door and seeing that look waiting for you. I knew immediately I was in for it.

"Uh, hi Mom. How are you?" I asked forcing my big brown eyes to become even bigger and using my most innocent voice. *(Why is the narrator using an innocent voice?)* Mom didn't answer. Instead, she just stared at me, shaking her head. She was a lioness ready to pounce, and I just needed to figure out which antic she found out about. *(What is an antic? It must be the reason the narrator was in trouble.)* I was pretty sure she couldn't have found out about my trip to the mall, but maybe it was what happened in math class. *(I wonder what happened at the mall? Was the narrator cheating in math?)*

What was going through your head as you read? Did you make a connection? Most of us have had an experience where we've been in big trouble with a parent. Did you have different questions pop into your head?

PRACTICE INTERACTING WITH TEXT

Read the next part of the story and try to interact with the text. Write your predictions, questions, connections, and comments in the margin. You will be able to write on the test, so practice this strategy now. Remember to slow down and really think about what you are reading.

"Would you like to explain this Connor?" Mom said as she waved an envelope between the two of us. "I don't understand why you keep getting into all this trouble." She continued to shout as the paper jabbed back and forth. She looked like a knight trying to slay the evil dragon.

I could tell from the envelope it had been mailed from Wilson Elementary School. I had erased the answering machine message from my math teacher and the one from the principal, too. I guess they finally mailed a letter home explaining why I had in-school suspension last week. I had to think fast. Maybe I could still get out of this.

"I can explain Mom," I quickly said. What now? How could I justify shooting spitballs at Jessica Johnson?

Although you have practiced writing down your thoughts, you will want to do these things in your head during the test. Writing them down will take too much time, but that doesn't mean you shouldn't be thinking them. Remember, your goal is to read and understand the text the **first** time. By using reading strategies, you will remember and understand more of the story. As a result, the questions will be much easier to answer. Read the passage below and practice your strategies in your head. If there is something that really stands out, feel free to underline or write on the text.

Then I blurted out, "I didn't do it!" As soon as the words flew out of my mouth I wanted to take them back. I knew I shouldn't have said it, but I couldn't help myself. Now I was really in for it. "It was Robbie! He sits next to me, and the teacher made a mistake. I didn't want to rat him out." I didn't know what was wrong with me. The lies were lava flowing from an active volcano. There was no stopping them.

"I'll take care of this immediately," my mom said with a sympathetic look on her face. Before I could protest, she picked up the phone and started to dial. I slunk into the chair, mortified, but not knowing what to say. I knew Robbie's mom wouldn't believe him, and he would be grounded for a month. I listened to my mom retell the story. Then she said the dreaded words. "I'm just disappointed that Robbie let Connor get in trouble for something he did." I couldn't take it any longer.

"Stop Mom! I did it! I was sitting behind Jessica and I was angry that she had gotten an A on the test. I thought it would be funny to shoot spitballs into her hair. She would leave the room with all the tiny pieces of paper stuck in her head and people would laugh. It was wrong! I know it was wrong!"

At that moment, my mom hung up the phone without saying another word. She had a knowing smile on her face and she said in a very calm voice, "Go to your room." It was at that moment that I realized my mom was smarter than I thought. She knew all along I was lying. She had never dialed Robbie's mom, and I had admitted everything. All I could do was accept the consequence. I knew I deserved whatever punishment she gave me, and I was sure it would be a biggie.

USING CONTEXT CLUES

As you read, you may get stuck on an unfamiliar word. Don't panic! Try to use context clues to figure it out. Let's go back to *The Look*. Reread the first sentence.

As I walked through the front door, I saw my mom standing in the foyer, her arms crossed, and the look I knew all too well on her face.

"Foyer" may be an unfamiliar word to you, but if you use the clues around it, you will probably be able to figure out its definition. Mom was standing in the foyer, so it sounds like a place, and the narrator saw Mom in the foyer as he walked through the front door. With these clues, the reader can make a guess that the foyer is the area of the house by the front door.

PRACTICE

Context Clues

Now, it's your turn to practice using context clues. Read each passage from the narrative above and try to figure out the definition of each underlined word. Then, explain your evidence. How do you know this is the definition? Check your answers in the back of the book when you are done.

1. Mom didn't answer. Instead, she just stared at me, shaking her head. She was a lioness ready to <u>pounce</u>, and I just needed to figure out which antic she found out about.

Clues:

_____

_____

_____

_____

Definition:

_____

_____

2. She continued to shout as the paper <u>jabbed</u> back and forth. She looked like a knight trying to slay the evil dragon.

Clues:

_____

_____

_____

_____

Definition:

_____

_____

(Answers on p. 160.)

UNDERSTANDING STORY ELEMENTS

To answer the questions on this part of the NJ ASK5, you will need to understand the elements of a story. Sometimes the test may use a different word than you would use, and it is just a matter of knowing test vocabulary. Let's take some time to examine each element.

THE SETTING

The setting determines when and where the story takes place. Sometimes the author describes the setting within the story, and sometimes you need to use the clues given to figure it out. This is an important element to the story because it can influence the tone or mood of the story. For example, if the author describes a dark, creaky, old house, with boarded up windows as the setting, it may create a scary tone and make the reader feel a little nervous.

Where does *The Look* take place?

_____

_____

Do we know when it takes place?

_____

_____

How do you know this information?

_____

_____

_____

_____

You probably said the story takes place at Connor's house, and you would be correct. The author never tells us exactly when the story takes place, but we can figure it out. Does it sound like the story is taking place a long time ago or far off in the future? There are telephones, and the characters talk like someone would talk today. As readers, we can determine that the story is realistic fiction and probably takes place in recent times.

THE CHARACTERS

The characters are who the story is about. The readers learn about each character through the character's actions, words, and thoughts. Again, the author may come right out and tell us about the character, but more often we need to figure it out from clues in the story. For example, if the author describes Connor slowly walking up to the old, creaky house with sweaty palms and a pale face, the readers can determine that Connor is scared. Let's think back to *The Look* one more time. Keep Connor's words, actions, and thoughts in mind as well as anything else the author revealed. List as many character traits as you can about the main character Connor:

_____

_____

_____

_____

You may have listed some things the author told the reader such as Connor has big brown eyes and is in elementary school. Hopefully you used some clues from the text to dig deeper into Connor's personality. You may have said he was mean because he was shooting spitballs at Jessica or that he was sneaky because he wasn't being honest with his mom.

As you read a story, you want to keep a few questions in mind to help you learn more about the character:

- What physical traits do I know about the character?

- What do the character's thoughts, words, and actions tell me?

- How has the character changed throughout the story?

These questions may give you insight into other parts of the story.

THE PLOT

The plot is the sequence of events in the story. The plot focuses on the conflict, or problem, and how the character will resolve this problem. The plot usually follows a set structure, which you may have seen.

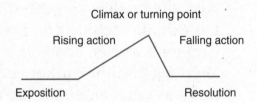

It begins with exposition, where the reader learns background information about the characters. It then moves to rising action. This is the biggest part of the story where the most action takes place. There are several events, each building with excitement and anticipation. This is the part of the story where the character encounters problems or complications. Each conflict, or problem, gives the readers insight into the character. The rising action leads to the point of the story where the character tries to resolve the problem. He or she makes a decision that will change the course of the story. This is the climax or turning point of the story. The events that happen after the climax are the falling action. These events lead up to the resolution. The resolution indicates how things will end up for the character.

When analyzing the plot ask yourself these questions:

- What is the conflict or problem of the story?

- What complications does the character face along the way?

- What is the turning point (the point of the story where the character's decision will lead towards some type of solution)?

- How is the conflict resolved?

Let's take a look at the plot to *The Look*.

PRACTICE

The Plot

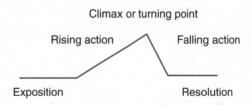

Exposition: What background information do we know?

_____

_____

Rising action: What happened to create the problem of the story? What events and complications happen in the story?

_____

_____

_____

_____

_____

Climax or turning point: In what part of the story does Connor make a decision that will change the course of the story?

_____

_____

_____

Falling action: What happens after the climax that will lead toward the resolution?

_____

_____

_____

Resolution: What will happen at the end of the story?

_____

_____

_____

_____

(Answers on pp. 160–161.)

THE THEME

Think of the theme as a life lesson. It is the moral or lesson the author would like the reader to learn. When trying to figure out the theme, you need to ask yourself the following questions:

- What does the author want the reader to learn from this story?

- How has the main character changed? What has he or she learned since the start of the story?

PRACTICE

The Theme

To find the theme of *The Look* ask yourself the following questions:

- What did Connor learn from this situation?

- What does the author want the reader to learn?

Write your answer on the lines below.

_____

_____

_____

_____

_____

_____

(Answers on p. 161.)

ANSWERING MULTIPLE-CHOICE QUESTIONS

After reading the passage, you will be faced with the multiple-choice questions. Again, you may be tempted to read these questions before you read the story. Do not do this! If you read the questions first, you are going to be looking for the answers and not paying attention to **all** of the text. You will need to understand **all** of the text to answer the open-ended questions that follow the multiple-choice questions. Instead, read the passage carefully, and use your reading strategies. Then, when you get to the multiple-choice, you will be prepared. Read the hints for answering multiple-choice questions, and then you'll have a chance to practice.

Hints for Multiple-Choice Questions

■ Start with the easy questions. Don't waste time on a question you don't know the answer to. Skip it and come back to it later, but be careful not to lose your place on the answer sheet. If you skip a question on the test, you need to skip that number when bubbling in the answers.

■ Circle key words in both the question and answers. You are allowed to write on the test, and often it helps!

■ Read the entire question and **all** of the answer choices. If more than one answer seems correct, check to see if there is an option for "all of the above." If there is not, then choose the best answer.

■ Use the process of elimination. Cross off answers that you know are incorrect.

■ Answer every question. Make a logical guess if you don't know the answer.

■ Don't try to be the first to finish! Check over your answers carefully when you are done.

PRACTICE

The Look—Multiple-Choice Questions

Reread the story from earlier in the chapter. Then, answer each multiple-choice question.

The Look

As I walked through the front door, I saw my mom standing in the foyer, her arms crossed, and the look I knew all too well on her face. It was the look that most mom's mastered early on in your childhood, the look that let you know to knock it off or else. The worst-case scenario was walking through the front door and seeing that look waiting for you. I knew immediately I was in for it.

"Uh, hi Mom. How are you?" I asked forcing my big brown eyes to become even bigger and using my most innocent voice. Mom didn't answer. Instead, she just stared at me, shaking her head. She was a lioness ready to pounce, and I just needed to figure out which antic she found out about. I was pretty sure she couldn't have found out about the mall, but maybe it was what happened in math class.

"Would you like to explain this Connor?" Mom said as she waved an envelope between the two of us. "I don't understand why you keep getting into all this trouble." She continued to shout as the paper jabbed back and forth. She looked like a knight trying to slay the evil dragon.

I could tell from the envelope it had been mailed from Wilson Elementary School. I had erased the answering machine message from my math teacher and the one from the principal, too. I guess they finally mailed a letter home explaining why I had in-school suspension last week. I had to think fast. Maybe I could still get out of this.

"I can explain Mom," I quickly said. What now? How could I justify shooting spitballs at Jessica Johnson?

Then I blurted out, "I didn't do it!" As soon as the words flew out of my mouth I wanted to take them back. I knew I shouldn't have said it, but I couldn't help myself. Now I was really in for it. "It was Robbie! He sits next to me, and the teacher made a mistake. I didn't want to rat him out." I didn't know what was wrong with me. The lies were lava flowing from an active volcano. There was no stopping them.

"I'll take care of this immediately," my mom said with a sympathetic look on her face. Before I could protest, she picked up the phone and started to dial. I slunk into the chair, mortified, but not knowing what to say. I knew Robbie's mom wouldn't believe him and he would be grounded for a month. I listened to my mom retell the story. Then she said the dreaded words. "I'm just disappointed that Robbie let Connor get in trouble for something he did." I couldn't take it any longer.

"Stop Mom! I did it! I was sitting behind Jessica and I was angry that she had gotten an A on the test. I thought it would be funny to shoot spitballs into her hair. She would leave the room with all the tiny pieces of paper stuck in her head and people would laugh. It was wrong! I know it was wrong!"

At that moment, my mom hung up the phone without saying another word. She had a knowing smile on her face and she said in a very calm voice, "Go to your room." It was at that moment that I realized my mom was smarter than I thought. She knew all along I was lying. She had never dialed Robbie's mom and I had admitted everything. All I could do was accept the consequence. I knew I deserved whatever punishment she gave me and I was sure it would be a biggie.

Multiple-Choice Questions

1. In the story the narrator describes his mom as "a lioness ready to pounce." How do you think the mom is feeling at this point of the story?

   A. Hungry

   B. Angry

   C. Sad

   D. Tired

2. Which of the following best describes the main character Connor?

   A. Trustworthy

   B. Funny

   C. Sneaky

   D. Happy

3. In the last paragraph, the word "consequence" means
_____.

   A. cause

   B. bad

   C. reward

   D. outcome or result of something that happened
      earlier

4. Why do you think Connor erased the messages on the
   answering machine?

   A. His mom had listened to them.

   B. He was going to tell his mom about the message.

   C. It was an accident.

   D. He was hiding them from his mom.

5. The lies were lava flowing from an active volcano is
   an example of _____.

   A. simile

   B. metaphor

   C. personification

   D. alliteration

(Answers on p. 161.)

ANSWERING AN OPEN-ENDED QUESTION

The last thing you will need to do with this story is to
answer the open-ended question. You will have one
question for each story you read. You may want to
consider answering the open-ended question before the
multiple-choice. Each question is worth a large number of
points, and if you are running out of time, there is no
guessing on an open-ended question. In contrast, you

could guess on the multiple-choice questions if time is running short.

Your response to the open-ended question will be scored using a four-point rubric designed by the state of New Jersey. Take a minute to look at the elements of the rubric.

Points	Criteria
4	A four-point response clearly demonstrates an understanding of the task, completes all requirements, and provides an insightful explanation/opinion that links to or extends aspects of the text.
3	A 3-point response demonstrates an understanding, completes all requirements, and provides some explanation/opinion using situations or ideas from the text as support.
2	A 2-point response may address all of the requirements, but demonstrates a partial understanding of the text, and uses text incorrectly or with limited success resulting in an inconsistent or flawed explanation.
1	A 1-point response demonstrates minimal understanding of the text, does not complete the requirements, and provides only a vague reference to or no use of the text.
0	A 0-point response is irrelevant or off topic.

What does all this mean? How can you actually score a 4 on this part of the test? To achieve this score you will need to provide an answer that is clear and answers the question completely. As the author, you must provide a meaningful explanation or opinion that uses text and extends past the text. This means that part of the answer relates to the text but comes from an outside source, such as a personal experience or a connection to other literature.

When completing the open-ended question, you will need to keep three things in mind: restate it, support it, and conclude it.

Restate it simply means to restate the question. Read the sample below to see how to restate the question.

Question: How was Connor feeling when his Mom was on the phone with Robbie's mom?

Restate it: Connor was feeling guilty when his Mom was on the phone with Robbie's mom.

The author simply turned the question into a sentence. "Guilty" could be replaced with another word of your choice, as long as you have evidence from the text to support your idea.

Next, you will need to support your answer. You must have evidence from the text, but you can also use evidence from your own life. For example, in the story Connor feels guilty. The reader knows this because he slunk into the chair, mortified and he interrupted his mom when she voiced her disappointment. This is the evidence I will use when I write my open-ended response. You might also use a personal connection as evidence. If you can connect to the question in a logical way, this is a great strategy for writing an open-ended response. If you do this, make sure you explain how your experience connects to the character or text.

Lastly, you need to conclude it. This means you need to write a concluding sentence that summarizes your thoughts. Now let's read the open-ended response that follows. In this answer the author restates it, supports it, and concludes it. Notice how the author uses a personal connection to enhance the evidence.

Connor was feeling guilty when his Mom was on the phone with Robbie's mom. This is evident because the author says Connor slunk down into his chair mortified. This sounds like he doesn't like what his mom is saying, and it's probably because he knows it's not true. When his mom says she's disappointed in Robbie, Connor breaks down and admits the truth. He doesn't want his friend to get in trouble for something he did. This proves that Connor was feeling guilty about what happened. I can relate to Connor because once I blamed my sister for something I did. When she was punished, I broke down and admitted the truth. I know the guilt that Connor must feel and know that he will probably learn a lesson from this experience.

PRACTICE

The Look—Open-Ended Question

Now it's your turn to give it a try. Read the following open-ended question and then write your answer on the lines provided. Compare your answer to the example in the back of the book.

(Answers on p. 162.)

Was it fair for Connor's mom to trick him into telling the truth? Use evidence from the text to support your answer.

Remember to restate it, support it, and conclude it.

Hints for Success

■ Do not read the questions before reading the story! Even though you might be tempted, you will need to read carefully in order to answer the open-ended questions well.

■ Slow down! It will benefit you to read using your strategies! Interact with the text. Ask questions and make predictions. Then read to see if you are right or wrong. Remember, your goal is to read and understand the text the first time! You can write on the test if this helps you.

■ Answer the open-ended question before the multiple-choice questions. If you are running out of time, you can guess at a multiple-choice question, but not the open-ended question.

■ Remember to restate it, support it, and conclude it when answering your open-ended question! You must use evidence from the text!

■ Apply strategies for answering multiple-choice questions. Read the entire question and all of the options, start with the easy questions, eliminate possibilities that you know are wrong, and write on the test.

■ Answer every question!

PRACTICE TIME!

Now it is your turn to practice! On the following pages, you will find a sample narrative passage. Make sure you read the directions carefully. You only have 30 minutes for this reading task. It is very important that you set a timer for yourself or ask someone to set the time for you. Good luck and remember to use all the hints you have learned so far! When you are finished, check your answers in the back of the book.

PRACTICE

Narrative Text

Directions: You will have 30 minutes to read the story and answer the questions. You may write on the test.

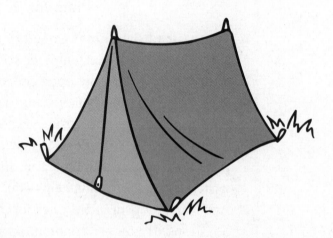

A Night to Remember

Abby collapsed onto the ground and began sobbing. How had she gotten herself into this mess? After several minutes, she picked herself up and leaned against the tree behind her. She stared up at the canopy of branches. Someone had to be out there looking for her. She turned her head to the right and listened intently. Then, she turned her head to the left and did the same thing. Her ears only found silence, but then she heard leaves rustling behind her. Abby's heart skipped a beat, and she jumped to her feet with a big smile on her face. "I'm over here!" she yelled. At that moment she realized it wasn't Mrs. Watts her scout leader or one of the other girls from her troop; it was just a deer looking for food. Abby burst into tears one more time, and the frightened deer took off into the woods.

Just two hours ago, Abby had been having fun with all her friends in troop 524. The ten girls in the troop had just gotten to Camp Bernie with the scout leader Mrs. Watts and Jenna's mom, Mrs. Johnson. The first thing they had to do was pitch their tents. It was a hard job, and Abby wasn't happy about it. "This is hard work," she complained to her best friend Jenna. "I shouldn't be sweating. This is supposed to be a vacation, right?"

"It won't take us too long," Jenna replied as she started to secure the tent to the stakes. Jenna camped with her family at least once a month.

"I know. I just thought we were going to have more fun on this trip," Abby replied. Abby was eleven years old, but this was her first time camping.

After the girls had all their tents pitched, it was time to start gathering firewood. They would need the fire to cook food and stay warm at night. "Everyone stick with at least one friend," Mrs. Watts instructed the girls, "and don't wander too far!"

At first, Abby headed off with Jenna and Tiffany. They found a few big pieces of wood, but then Abby saw a really cool grouping of rocks just up the hill. It looked like the perfect place to plop down and relax. I'll check it out and then tell Jenna and Tiffany. It can be our secret hangout while we're camping this weekend. Abby started heading up the hill towards the cluster of rocks. She had to keep looking down to make sure she didn't fall, and after a while, when she looked up, the rocks were nowhere to be found. I thought I was heading right towards them, Abby thought to herself.

Now, here she was, alone and crying in the woods. The sun was starting to set and the temperature was dropping. Abby didn't know what to do. She thought back to what Mrs. Watts always told them in scouts, "If you ever get lost, you should stay in one place."

Abby knew what she had to do but it was getting cold, and she had no fire. I'll try to gather some branches to use as shelter, she thought to herself. For about an hour, Abby worked hard to lean branches and leaves between two trees. She layered as many leaves on the ground as she could and then settled herself in to wait for someone to find her. As the sun set, she heard rustling behind her again. Only this time she also heard sniffing and scratching. Abby froze, her eyes wide. She heard the rustling getting closer to her. Abby's hands began to sweat despite the cold temperatures. Don't move, and it will go away, Abby thought to herself as she clenched her big eyes shut and became a statue. After what seemed to be a millennium, the sounds started to drift further and further away. A sigh of relief escaped Abby's chest and she took a few deep breaths.

It was at that moment that Abby saw a dull light in the distance. Could it be a flashlight? Abby took a chance and began yelling, "Help, I'm over here!" The lights began to get closer and closer. Abby jumped to her feet. It was really happening. Someone was coming to save her. Just then Mrs. Watts, Jenna, and Tiffany appeared from behind a tree. Tears ran down Abby's face, and she sprinted toward them. When she reached her scout leader and friends, she gave them each a hug. "I'm so sorry," she said. "I didn't mean to disappear. It was an accident." She tried to catch her breath but she was crying so hard it was difficult.

"I'm glad you're okay, but I hope you learned your lesson, Abby," Mrs. Watts said with a slight scowl on her face.

"It won't happen again. I promise," Abby replied.

When the group got back to camp, dinner was ready and waiting for them. When the meal was over, Abby was the first to jump up. "I'll do all the dishes," she said and before anyone could say anything she collected the plates and began cleaning up.

Multiple-Choice Questions

Choose the best answer for each multiple-choice question.

1. In paragraph one, Abby listens intently. "Intently" means _____.

   A. with great attention

   B. quietly

   C. with anticipation

   D. with hope

2. In the first paragraph, how did Abby feel when she heard leaves rustling ?

   A. Scared

   B. Lonely

   C. Excited

   D. Sad

3. According to the text, why was it important for the girls to gather wood for a fire?

   A. To cook food

   B. To stay warm

   C. To scare animals away

   D. Both A and B

4. What rule does Mrs. Watts give the scouts before they start gathering wood?

   A. Stay with at least one friend.

   B. Bring water.

   C. Don't wander too far.

   D. Both A and C.

5. Where was Abby heading when she got lost?

   A. To the top of the mountain

   B. Down the hill

   C. Back to camp

   D. To a cluster of rocks

6. How did Abby prepare for her night lost in the woods?

   A. She built a fire.

   B. She used branches and leaves for a shelter.

   C. She gathered food.

   D. Both A and B.

7. How did Abby know help was coming?

   A. She heard leaves rustling.

   B. She heard sirens.

   C. She saw light.

   D. She heard people calling her name.

8. How did Mrs. Watts feel when they finally found Abby?

    A. Happy

    B. Surprised they had found her

    C. Relieved but angry

    D. None of the above

9. The metaphor Abby was a statue means Abby was _____.

    A. still

    B. tough

    C. strong

    D. none of the above

10. The best theme statement for this story is _____.

    A. Be a good friend.

    B. Camping can be dangerous.

    C. Camping is fun.

    D. Hard work pays off.

Open-Ended Question

11. In the story, Abby has a frightening experience while camping. How has Abby's opinion about camping changed? Use evidence from the text to support your answer.

_____

_____

_____

_____

_____

_____

_____

_____

_____

_____

_____

_____

_____

_____

_____

_____

(Answers on pp. 162–164.)

READING EVERYDAY TEXT

WHAT IS EVERDAY TEXT?

The second type of text you will see on the NJ ASK5 is called everyday text. Think about the text you encounter on a daily basis. What do you see? You might read novels or stories, which would be narrative text. You might also see newspapers, magazine articles, textbooks, letters, or directions. These would be examples of everyday text. Everyday text is expository or persuasive writing, which means the author's purpose is to explain, inform, or persuade the reader.

READING FOR UNDERSTANDING

When we read narrative text, we practiced interacting with the story. As we read everyday text, we want to continue stopping to use reading strategies. Although this will slow your reading slightly, it will allow you to understand and remember more information the first time you read it. You have only 30 minutes for this section of the test, so you don't want to waste time rereading the passage. Take a minute to review the strategies from the last chapter.

Reading Strategies

■ Predict—Make a guess about what will happen in the article.
■ Question—Ask questions of the author and text.
■ Connect—Make connections between the text and your life, other text, or the world.
■ Summarize—Stop periodically and retell what has happened so far in the article.
■ Visualize—Create a mental picture of what is happening.
■ Context clues—If you don't know a word, use the words around it to try to figure it out.

With everyday text, summarizing is going to be a very important strategy. You need to stop periodically and make sure you can retell what you have read. By doing this, you are testing yourself for understanding. Let's give it a try. Read the first paragraph and pay attention to my thoughts in parentheses. Then, you'll have a chance to try this on your own.

School Lunches: Are They Healthy?

Cafeteria lunches have gotten a bad rap for years. *(The cafeteria lunches aren't very good in my school.)* The typical lunch lady, wearing a hair net and plopping unrecognizable food onto every kid's tray. *(I've seen this in movies, but our lunch ladies don't look like this.)* Luckily, this is not the case in many school cafeterias today. Now, with new health regulations, *(What does "regulations" mean?)* food has become healthier and in many cases better. *(If regulations made it healthier, maybe it means rules.)* Yet, there is still debate among students about whether these new regulations are fair and among parents about whether these regulations work. Students feel they are old enough to make their own food choices *(Some kids might be old enough.)* and don't agree with the government mandating the food they eat. They miss real potato chips, greasy French fries, and sugary drinks. Parents are finding out their kids are still not eating healthy meals despite regulations by the New Jersey government. *(If there are rules, why aren't they eating healthier meals?)* As a result, it is time to evaluate the food being served in school cafeterias. *(It sounds like the article will talk about why there should and shouldn't be food regulations in school cafeterias.)*

What was going through your head as you read? Write down questions, connections, or any other thoughts that popped into your head as you read the paragraph.

_____

_____

_____

_____

What strategies did you see used in the sample?

_X_ Predict—The reader predicted what the article would be about.

_X_ Question—The reader questioned why kids aren't eating healthier if there are rules.

 X Connect—The reader connected to the cafeteria in his or her own school as well as movies he or she had seen that featured lunch ladies.

___ Summarize—The author did not summarize.

___ Visualize—The author did not visualize.

 X Context clues—The author used context clues to figure out the word "regulation."

The author did not summarize yet, but we know this is a really important strategy to use when reading this type of text. How could we summarize this paragraph? Let's read it one more time and look for key words. Then, we'll try to rewrite the paragraph in just a sentence or two.

School Lunches: Are They Healthy?

Cafeteria lunches have gotten a bad rap for years. The typical lunch lady, wearing a hair net and plopping unrecognizable food onto every kid's tray. Luckily, this is not the case in many school cafeterias today. Now, with new health regulations, food has become healthier and in many cases better. Yet, there is still debate among students about whether these new regulations are fair and among parents about whether these regulations work. Students feel they are old enough to make their own food choices and don't agree with the government mandating the food they eat. They miss real potato chips, greasy French fries, and sugary drinks. Parents are finding out their kids are still not eating healthy meals despite regulations by the New Jersey government. As a result, it is time to evaluate the food being served in school cafeterias.

Let's take these ideas and put them into one or two sentences.

Although New Jersey regulates the food served in school cafeterias, it is unclear whether the regulations are helping kids eat healthier. Kids and parents disagree, so schools will need to evaluate the food being served.

PRACTICE INTERACTING WITH TEXT

It's your turn to give it a try. Read the next paragraph of the article. Remember, to stop yourself and interact with the text. Ask questions, make connections, react to the text, and summarize. When you are finished, try to write a one or two sentence summary of the paragraph. Your goal is to train yourself to do these things as you read. By using these strategies, you will understand and remember more of the text. Write on the text if it helps you.

When kids step into the cafeteria line, they are offered a well-balanced meal. Food from every food group comprises a complete lunch. Unfortunately, this is not the choice most students make. Instead of chicken, potatoes, corn, fruit, and milk, many trays have multiple packs of baked chips and low-fat cookies. Is this a healthier choice for kids? Too much of even these lighter versions are still not nutritious options for kids. Children need nutrient-rich foods to help their developing bodies grow healthily.

What strategies did you use as you read this paragraph?

___ Predict—Make predictions about what will happen in the article.

___ Question—Ask questions of the author and text.

___ Connect—Make connections between the text and your life, other text, or the world.

___ Summarize—Stop periodically and retell what has happened so far in the article.

___ Visualize—Create a mental picture of what is happening.

___ Context clues—If you don't know a word, use the words around it to try and figure it out.

How did you summarize this paragraph? Write one or two sentences to explain what this paragraph is about.

_____

_____

_____

_____

_____

UNDERSTANDING EXPOSITORY TEXT STRUCTURE

Most of the time everyday text, or expository text, follows an expected three-part structure. The first part is the introduction, which is typically the first paragraph of the text. Here the author grabs the readers' attention and lets them know what to expect in the article, essay, letter, or other text. The second part of the structure is the body of the text. This is the biggest part of the writing and the place where readers will gather the most information. This is where the author will explain, inform, or persuade the readers by using evidence and examples to support his or her point. Lastly, the author will conclude his or her writing. This is usually the last paragraph of the text. The author will remind the readers of his or her point and leave them with something to think about.

FINDING THE THESIS

The thesis, or main idea, is very important to this type of writing. It is usually found in the first paragraph and tells readers what the text will be about. Often, the author will tell readers the thesis statement, but sometimes it is implied. This means the author doesn't come right out and tell the reader but instead gives clues in order for readers to figure out the topic of the writing.

PRACTICE

Identifying the Thesis Statement

We're going to look at a few examples. Read each paragraph below. Then try to figure out the thesis statement. Ask yourself, what is this text going to be about? What is the author going to write about in this article?

Paragraph 1

Many people claim that dog is man's best friend. Over time, dogs have helped people find food and protect their homes. Most importantly, dogs are companions for many people. Yet, others will argue that dogs can be dangerous, are expensive, and represent lots of work. These people will say if you are looking for good company, then you are looking for a cat. Cats are easy to take care of and reliable. As you decide the best pet for you and your family, you will need to weigh the positives and negatives of owning either a dog or a cat.

What is the thesis statement? Ask yourself, what will this article be about?

_____

_____

_____

Paragraph 2

Meggy's dad, Chris, sat wheezing in the chair watching television. He had been out of work for the past six months because of lung cancer, and the family could barely afford to pay the monthly bills. Chris had started smoking as a teenager, and now 20 years later he was paying the price. Although the number of teens who smoke has recently decreased, it is still a prevalent problem in America. In 2008, one in eight high school seniors were smoking cigarettes, which is still way too many.

What is the thesis statement? Ask yourself, what will this article be about?

_____

_____

_____

(Answers on p. 164.)

ANSWERING MULTIPLE-CHOICE QUESTIONS

After reading the text, you will answer multiple-choice questions. Again, you might be tempted to read the questions before you read the passage. Do not do this! When you read the questions first, you tend to read for the answers and miss information. To answer the open-ended question, you will need to understand all of the text. It is better to read and use your strategies the first time, so you don't have to reread and waste time. Take a minute to review hints for answering the multiple-choice questions.

Hints for Multiple-Choice Questions

■ Start with the easy questions. Don't waste time on a question you don't know the answer to. Skip it and come back to it later, but be careful not to lose your place on the answer sheet. If you skip a question on the test, you need to skip that number when bubbling in the answers.

■ Circle key words in both the question and answers. You are allowed to write on the test, and often it helps!

■ Read the entire question and all of the answer choices. If more than one answer seems correct, check to see if there is an option for "all of the above." If there is not, then choose the best answer.

■ Use the process of elimination. Cross off answers that you know are incorrect.

■ Answer every question. Make a logical guess if you don't know the answer.

■ Don't try to be the first to finish! Check over your answers carefully when you are done.

PRACTICE

School Lunches: Are They Healthy—Multiple-Choice Questions

Read the complete article *School Lunches: Are They Healthy?* and apply your reading strategies. Remember, you can write on the text. Then answer the multiple-choice questions. When you are finished, check your answers at the end of the book.

School Lunches: Are They Healthy?

Cafeteria lunches have gotten a bad rap for years. The typical lunch lady, wearing a hair net and plopping unrecognizable food onto every kid's tray. Luckily, this is not the case in many school cafeterias today. Now, with new health regulations, food has become healthier and in many cases better. Yet, there is still debate among students about whether these new regulations are fair and among parents about whether these regulations work. Students feel they are old enough to make their own food choices and don't agree with the government mandating the food they eat. They miss real potato chips, greasy French fries, and sugary drinks. Parents are finding out their kids are still not eating healthy meals despite regulations by the New Jersey government. As a result, it is time to evaluate the food being served in school cafeterias.

When kids step into the cafeteria line they are offered a well-balanced meal. Food from every food group comprises a complete lunch. Unfortunately, this is not the choice most students make. Instead of chicken, potatoes, corn, fruit, and milk, many trays have multiple packs of baked chips and low-fat cookies. Is this a healthier choice for kids? Too much of even these lighter versions are still not nutritious options for kids. Children need nutrient-rich foods to help their developing bodies grow healthily.

Many parents are unaware of the food being eaten by their children at school. They assume their son or daughter is eating a healthy, well-balanced meal. Samantha, a fifth grader, reported eating pizza and chips every day for lunch. When asked about the complete lunch offered, including fruit and vegetable, she replied, "No one eats that! I don't know why they even offer it." Therefore, the government needs to question if these regulations are worth having in place if kids are rejecting them and schools aren't enforcing them.

On the contrary, childhood obesity is on the rise and kids aren't taking control of the problem themselves. Therefore, adults need to intervene and help solve this problem. Today, more than 9 million kids between the ages of 6 and 19 are either overweight or obese, and this number keeps rising. It has more than doubled over the past 3 years. Furthermore, 70 percent of these obese children will become obese adults and these children are at a greater risk for heart disease, diabetes, and cancer later in life.

The question remains, should food regulations exist for schools and are these regulations working? Will this action help reduce obesity in kids today? Perhaps parents, teachers, and school administrators need to think further about how to help kids make the right choices. Until children can make good food choices independently, the problem will not be resolved.

Multiple-Choice Questions

1. Which sentence is the best thesis statement?

    A. Schools should monitor the foods kids eat.

    B. Schools should not monitor the foods kids eat.

    C. It is time to evaluate the food being served in school cafeterias.

    D. Kids should make their own food choices.

2. Kids don't agree with the government mandating cafeteria food. What does "mandating" mean?

    A. Free choice

    B. Keep food fresh

    C. Allow for snacks

    D. To order or require

3. According to the article, why do kids think they should have free choice of foods in the cafeteria?

   A. They are paying for it.

   B. They are old enough to make their own decisions.

   C. Adults choose their own foods.

   D. Kids in other states choose their own foods.

4. Why don't children eat the well-balanced meal offered in the cafeteria?

   A. Kids choose to eat the snacks instead.

   B. They bring lunches from home.

   C. The food doesn't taste good.

   D. They choose not to eat lunch.

5. How many kids today are overweight or obese?

   A. More than 3 million

   B. More than 9 million

   C. More than 12 million

   D. More than 1 million

6. How can childhood obesity impact kids when they are adults?

   A. Greater risk for heart disease

   B. Greater risk for diabetes

   C. Greater risk for cancer

   D. All of the above

(Answers on pp. 164–165.)

ANSWERING AN OPEN-ENDED QUESTION

The last thing to do in this portion of the test is to answer an open-ended question. Remember, an open-ended question means you cannot simply answer yes or no; instead, you need to offer an explanation and evidence to support your answer. Again, you may want to consider answering the open-ended question before the multiple-choice questions. The open-ended question is worth a large number of points, and if you are running out of time, there is no guessing on an open-ended question. In contrast, you could guess on the multiple-choice question if you needed to.

Your open-ended response will be scored using the same four-point rubric we used for narrative text. Take a minute to review the elements of the rubric.

Points	Criteria
4	A 4-point response clearly demonstrates an understanding of the task, completes all requirements, and provides an insightful explanation/opinion that links to or extends aspects of the text.
3	A 3-point response demonstrates an understanding, completes all requirements, and provides some explanation/opinion using situations or ideas from the text as support.
2	A 2-point response may address all of the requirements, but demonstrates a partial understanding of the text, and uses text incorrectly or with limited success resulting in an inconsistent or flawed explanation.
1	A 1-point response demonstrates minimal understanding of the text, does not complete the requirements, and provides only a vague reference to or no use of the text.
0	A 0-point response is irrelevant or off topic.

Your goal is to achieve a 4 on this part of the test. To do this, you will need to provide an answer that is clear and completely answers the question. As the author, you must provide a meaningful explanation or opinion that uses text and extends past the text. This means that part of the answer relates to the text but comes from an outside source, such as a personal connection.

As with the narrative open-ended question, you will need to keep three things in mind: restate it, support it, and conclude it. Let's start by restating the question. We need to turn the question into a statement. Look at the question below, and notice how we can turn it into the first sentence of our paragraph.

> **Question:** Are fifth graders old enough to make their own food choices while at school? Use evidence from the text to support your answer.
>
> **Restate it:** Fifth graders are old enough to make their own food choices while at school.
>
> or
>
> Fifth graders are not old enough to make their own food choices in the cafeteria.

All we needed to do was turn the question into a statement. It is simple and to the point. Next, you will need to support your answer. You must have evidence from the text but can also use evidence from your own life. For example, if my topic sentence is "Fifth graders are not old enough to make their own food choices," my evidence might be that there are more than 9 million obese kids. In addition, I could use Samantha's quote that no one actually eats the complete lunch. Lastly, the author needs to conclude it. This means the author must write a concluding sentence to summarize his or her thoughts. Now let's read the open-ended response. In this answer the author restates it, supports it, and concludes it. Notice how the author uses a personal connection to enhance the evidence.

Fifth graders are not old enough to make their own food choices at school. If kids could make healthy choices on their own, there would not be so many obese children. There are currently more than nine million obese kids in America, which is way too many. In addition, kids will come right out and tell you that they don't eat the complete lunch designed by the cafeteria. Instead, they fill up on snacks. I see the poor choices kids make in my school. Even though the cafeteria serves baked chips, it is still not healthy if someone only eats four bags of chips for lunch, and this is what many kids are doing. In conclusion, fifth graders are not old enough to make their own food choices and should either bring a lunch prepared by their parents or eat a lunch set by the school. This would definitely reduce obesity and help kids become healthier.

PRACTICE

School Lunches: Are They Healthy?—Open-Ended Question

Now it's your turn to give it a try. Read the following open-ended question and then write your answer on the lines provided. Remember to restate it, support it, and conclude it. When you are finished, compare your answer to the example in the back of the book.

> Are school lunches healthier for kids now that there are rules to follow? Should New Jersey continue to regulate cafeteria lunches?

_____

_____

_____

_____

_____

_____

_____

_____

_____

_____

_____

_____

_____

_____

_____

_____

_____

_____

(Answers on p. 165.)

Hints for Success

- Do not read the questions before reading the article! Even though you might be tempted, you will need to read carefully in order to answer the open-ended question well.
- Slow down! It will benefit you to read using your strategies! Interact with the text. Ask questions and make predictions. Then, read to see if you are right or wrong. Remember, your goal is to read and understand the text the first time!
- Answer the open-ended question before the multiple-choice questions. If you are running out of time, you can guess at a multiple-choice question, but not the open-ended question.
- Remember to restate it, support it, and conclude it when answering your open-ended question! You must use evidence from the text!
- Apply strategies for answering multiple-choice questions. Read the entire question and all of the options, start with the easy questions, eliminate possibilities that you know are wrong, and write on the test.
- Answer every question!

PRACTICE TIME!

Now it is your turn to practice on your own! On the following pages, you will find a sample everyday text passage. Make sure you read the directions carefully. You have only 30 minutes for this reading task. It is very important that you set a timer for yourself or ask someone to set the time for you. Good luck and remember to use all the hints you have learned! When you are finished, check your answers in the back of the book.

PRACTICE

Expository Text

Video Games: Helping or Hurting Kids Today

According to CNN Health, approximately 90 percent of kids between the ages of 8 and 16 spend about 13 hours a week playing video games. This excessive amount of time spent in front of a gaming system causes concern among many parents. Adults fear their children will become more violent because of the video games they play. Some parents forbid their children from playing certain games, and others want state legislature to pass laws further regulating video games. Contrary, there are some benefits to children playing video games. Not only can they teach logic and problem solving skills, they also teach kids how to follow directions. Therefore, the question remains: do the benefits of video games outweigh the dangers?

Most kids will argue that video games are fun and worth playing. The overall opinion of American youth is that they will not make kids violent. Cameron, a fifth grader in South Bound Brook, claims that all of his friends play video games and it

doesn't make them angry or aggressive. "Movies might influence kids to do bad things, but everyone knows video games are just for fun." However, recent studies published by the *American Pediatric Journal* found both American and Japanese children who play violent video games show greater signs of aggression. The study compared the number of hours children spent playing violent video games to aggressive behaviors, which included hitting, kicking, and fighting other kids. The study proved that younger children were more influenced than older kids by video games.

John, a fifth grader in Hamilton Township, agrees with the findings. "Sometimes kids in school fight with each other, and they use moves from video games. They think they can beat anyone just because they are good at a game." This mentality in today's youth is the cause of concern for many adults.

One solution to keep young children safe was to rate video games. If a video game is rated M for mature, stores cannot sell it to minors. Unfortunately, this doesn't always keep young children from playing the games. Older siblings, relatives, and sometimes even parents allow children to watch and play these aggressive games. In order for society to have less violent children, parent need to monitor kids and make sure they are playing appropriate games. Appropriate games can offer valuable learning for today's youth. James Gee, a professor of learning sciences at the University of Wisconsin, found that video games actually boost brainpower. Gee claims, "We had a hard time finding kids who were bad at school but good at games."

Additionally, exercise can be a benefit of video games today. The Nintendo Wii allows for people to physically take part in games. With this console, participants box, play tennis, bowl, and much more. Although the activity is not equivalent to actively taking part in the real-life sport, it certainly is better than sitting around watching TV or playing a more sedentary game.

In the end, parents need to find a way for kids to benefit from the positive aspects of gaming without becoming overly aggressive. With proper supervision and support from adults and responsibility from children, it is possible to accomplish both. The goal is to maximize the technology available today while keeping kids safe.

Multiple-Choice Questions

1. How many hours do most kids spend playing video games in one week?

   A. 8

   B. 16

   C. 90

   D. 13

2. In paragraph one the author states, "This excessive amount of time spent in front of a gaming system causes concern among many parents." What does "excessive" mean?

   A. Fun

   B. Beyond the normal amount

   C. Less than usual

   D. Exciting

3. The article talks frequently about aggression. What is the best definition of aggression?

   A. Deliberate, unfriendly behavior

   B. Playing video games

   C. Acting as a loner

   D. None of the above

4. What were the results of the study examining both Japanese and American kids who play violent video games?

   A. Kids who play violent video games show more aggression.

   B. Older children were more influenced than younger children.

   C. Younger children were more influenced than older children.

   D. Both A and C

5. What was defined as an aggressive behavior in the study?

   A. Hitting

   B. Kicking

   C. Fighting other kids

   D. All of the above

6. How has the government attempted to make gaming safer for children?

   A. Pulled violent video games off the shelf

   B. Passed laws to stop violent games from being made

   C. Rated violent video games M for mature

   D. Forced parents who let their kids play violent games to pay a fine

7. Which of the following is NOT a benefit of video games?

   A. Teach logic and problem solving skills

   B. Allow kids to exercise

   C. Teach kids how to fight

   D. Teach hand–eye coordination

8. Professor Gee claims, "We had a hard time finding kids who were bad at school but good at games." What conclusion can you draw from this statement?

   A. Kids who play video games learn how to think and do well in school.

   B. Kids who play video games don't do their homework.

   C. Kids who play video games are loners.

   D. All of the above

9. The main idea of this article is _____.

   A. children should never play video games

   B. only teenagers should play video games

   C. video games will harm kids

   D. there are advantages and disadvantages to playing video games

Open-Ended Question

10. Do children spend too much time playing video games? How might this impact kids? Use evidence from the text to support your answer.

   _____

   _____

   _____

_____

_____

_____

_____

_____

_____

_____

_____

_____

_____

_____

_____

_____

_____

_____

_____

_____

(Answers on pp. 166–167.)

Chapter 4

SPECULATIVE WRITING

WHAT IS SPECULATIVE WRITING?

A speculative prompt? That sounds a little scary. How could the NJ ASK5 have a part whose title is hard to understand? It really is very easy. The great thing is that you speculate every day. Speculate means to take a guess about what would happen even if you do not have proof. So, if you were asked by your parents, "What would your perfect birthday dinner be?" you would be able to answer that easily. A prompt is a sentence or question that helps you think about your writing. If you put them together, a speculative prompt is a question that asks you to guess or imagine what will happen. You then write a story about it.

Here is an example. The NJ ASK5 could give you the following instructions. "If you could spend a day with any character from a book, who would it be? Write a story about your day with the character." Anyone can answer this question. You speculate, or think, about the character you would want to spend the day with. The prompt gives you the instructions (write a story). You will have 30 minutes to complete this task on the test.

On this part of the NJ ASK5, you will be a speculator. A long time ago in the western United States people searched for gold. These people were speculators. They did not know where the gold was, but they took a guess. When you are given a writing task you will plan out your guess and write a story.

The speculative prompt is not nearly as scary as it sounds. You will use the information in this chapter to write a story that meets all of the requirements you need to earn a top score. Now let's find our gold!

GENERATING YOUR IDEA

The first step to writing a story is coming up with your idea. This will be based on the prompt, or situation, given to you, and the story pie will help you keep track of the details. Good writing happens with good prewriting, so remember to take the first 5 minutes to really think your story through! Let's take a look at each slice of the story pie.

STORY PIE

Every piece of the pie helps create a good story!

Setting: Where and when does the story take place?

Give as many details as you can about the setting of the story

Character: What are the physical and personality traits of the characters?

How old is your main character? What does he or she look like? How does he or she behave and talk?

Conflict: What is the problem of the story?

Every story needs a good problem. Without an interesting conflict you have a boring story. What problem is your character faced with?

Resolution: How is the problem solved?

Your conflict needs to be resolved within the story. Don't make it too easy for the main characters to solve their problem. You will have a more interesting story if there is a complication along the way.

Theme: What lesson or moral would you like to teach the reader?

An author tells a story to teach the reader a lesson. What do you want the reader to learn from your story?

Story pie is quick to draw and allows you to think of the essential story elements **before** you begin writing. With this tool, prewriting will be easy as pie! The first slice is the **setting**. You want to have a good idea of when and where your story takes place. Think about the time period as well as the sensory details that surround your setting. Confused about sensory details? You have five senses—seeing, hearing, smelling, touching, and tasting. When an author writes descriptions focusing on the senses, it allows the reader to feel like they are a part of the story. It makes the writing vivid! When you are working on your prewrite, keep the sensory details in mind. Is it cold or hot and humid? Is it crowded or desolate?

The second slice of the pie describes your **main characters**. Who is this story about? Really think about your characters. Just writing a name is **not** good enough! A good author tells a story through the thoughts, words, and actions of their characters. In order to do this, you need to know your characters.

The **conflict**, or problem, is the third slice of the pie. **Every** story **must** have a problem. Often, with a speculative prompt you are given part of the problem and you might just need to add more information. When you are writing the problem, you want it to be a significant problem. It can't have too simple of a fix. You want your character to have to work a little to solve the problem; otherwise, you will have a **boring** story.

The final slice is the **resolution**, or the solution to the problem. How will your conflict be resolved? Again, this shouldn't be done too easily otherwise you don't have much of a story. If the problem is Joey lost his sock, and the solution is he walked to the store and bought a new pair of socks, your readers are probably going to be bored out of their minds. Who wants to read a story that isn't exciting? Readers want to see the characters have a challenge.

All of these slices of pie sit upon the theme. What is the theme? The theme is the lesson the author would like to teach the reader. Every good story teaches a lesson. Think about the stories you have read or heard. You may have learned to not lie, to listen to your parents, or to be kind to others. All of these life lessons are themes. When you are writing your story, you will need to think about the lesson you want the reader to learn.

Look at the following example to see how story pie can help you find the ingredients for a successful piece of writing!

Speculative Prompt

Emily has been waiting for a month to go on vacation with her family. The day has finally arrived and her family is at their destination. While unpacking, Emily realizes she forgot an important item. Write a story about the item Emily forgot and how it affects her vacation.

STORY PIE

Every piece of the pie helps create a good story!

Setting: Where and when does the story take place?

Present time
Month of May
Williamsburg, Virginia

Character: What are the physical and personality traits of the characters?

Emily is 11 years old
She is stubborn and gets angry if she doesn't get her way
Emily has brown hair and brown eyes

Conflict: What is the problem of the story?
Emily left her writing journal at home. Since she is missing school, her teacher told her she must keep a journal of her trip and record what she learns. Her family is only going to the amusement park once her work is done.

Resolution: How is the problem solved?
When Emily's parents ask if she has done her work, Emily lies and says it is done. Her parents ask to see it. Emily tells the truth. Her parents are angry but together they decide Emily could make a video journal. The family has fun making the video as they learn about Williamsburg. Emily apologizes, and they all have fun at the amusement park.

Theme: What lesson or moral would you like to teach the reader?

Be honest in life.

After completing this quick prewrite, it will be easy to write a detailed story. Remember, you have only 30 minutes for this part of the test. If you don't know where your story is headed, you will probably have a difficult time finishing. Prewriting will make this part of the test much easier!

PRACTICE

Prewriting

Now it's your turn! What will you have Emily forget? Where is she going? How will it impact her trip? How old is Emily? What type of personality does she have? It's all up to you!

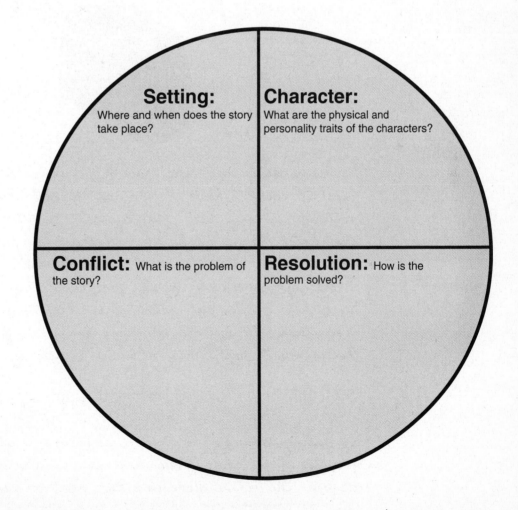

> **Theme:** What lesson or moral would you like to teach the reader?

OPENING YOUR STORY

Once you've finished your prewrite, it's time to write a draft. One of the easiest ways to make the reader want to read your story is to have a gripping opening, or lead. You can do this in many different ways! You'll need to experiment a little and find out what works for you.

An easy way to begin is to start off with the character thinking, saying, or doing something. Perhaps Emily might be thinking at the beginning of our story:

Mom and Dad are going to ground me for life! I must have left that dumb journal sitting on my bed. Emily sat in the middle of the hotel room with her suitcase dumped out around her. Her journal was the one thing she REALLY needed to pack for this trip. Not only were her grades at risk, but her trip to ride Mountain Adventure at the Great Virginia Amusement Park was also in jeopardy.

Or maybe we should start with Emily in action:

Emily dumped out her suitcase and searched frantically. She threw her new pink bathing suit across the room followed by her yellow sundress and the matching flip-flops. She tore through each piece of clothes before burying her face into the pillow of the hotel bed. Tears poured out of her brown eyes. "Forgetting that journal is going to ruin my vacation," Emily mumbled to herself.

Another way to begin your story is with a vivid description. If you use this strategy, you will want to focus on the sensory details. What does the setting look like, sound like, or feel like? Let's look at our story about Emily one more time:

As Emily stared out the window, she focused on the mountainous roller coaster ahead of her. The bright, yellow car slowly crept up the never-ending hill, and she could faintly hear the clicking in the distance. Just as the car flew down the steep hill, it hit her. She might not ever get to ride this incredible roller coaster because she had made a HUGE mistake! She had forgotten to pack the one thing she needed most on this trip to Williamsburg, Virginia.

PRACTICE

Opening Your Story

Now it's your turn. Look back at your own prewriting for this story. How will you grab the reader's attention and start your story? Use the space below to practice.

I will begin with: _____ the character speaking
_____ the character thinking
_____ the character in action
_____ a vivid description

_____

_____

_____

_____

_____

_____

_____

_____

_____

_____

_____

DETAILS, DETAILS, DETAILS

As you develop your story, you will want to include detailed sentences. By adding adjectives and adverbs, you can create a more descriptive piece of writing. What is the job of an adjective? An **adjective** describes a noun. For example, roller coaster is a noun. If I wanted to describe this roller coaster I would need to use adjectives like *tall*, *fast*, *scary*, or *amazing*. An **adverb** has the same job as an adjective, only it describes a verb. For example, if I wanted to describe how Emily looked for the journal in her suitcase, I could say she *frantically looked*, *desperately looked*, or *quickly looked*. Frantically, desperately, and quickly are my adverbs. They all describe the verb looked.

In addition to great word choice, an author wants to make the readers feel as if they are part of the story. How are you going to do this? Show, don't tell techniques are your answer! Show, don't tell simply means that you want to describe what is happening in the scene. For example, instead of just saying Emily was upset, we can say Emily slouched back onto the bed defeated. The tears began to pour out of her eyes as she held her head in her hands. Now, we've **shown** how Emily is feeling rather than just saying she's sad. It's your turn to give this a try.

Let's revise some simple, boring sentences into more descriptive sentences. Read each of the sentences below. Then, try to add adjectives and adverbs to make them more vivid. Keep word choice in mind as you revise. Are there more sophisticated or meaningful words to use? Remember, you want to show, not tell the details. Look at the example below:

> **Original writing:** Emily ran toward the roller coaster. She was nervous and excited.
>
> **Revised writing:** Emily sprinted toward the huge roller coaster. Her smile filled her face, and she could feel her heart beating in her chest. As she reached the line, Emily looked up at the steep hill above her and felt the flutters in her stomach.

PRACTICE

Adding Details

Read each sentence. Then revise for better word choice and to add details.

Emily looked through her suitcase for the journal.

_____

_____

_____

_____

_____

Emily walked into her parents' room and admitted she forgot her journal at home.

_____

_____

_____

_____

_____

Maybe the middle of your story will look something like this:

What was she going to do? Emily was missing school to go on this trip with her family, and she had to do her work before she was allowed to go to the amusement park. Her teacher gave Emily a journal to write down everything that happened to her on the trip. How was she going to do her work if she didn't have the journal?

"Emily?" Emily's mom called from the other room of the hotel.

"Yes, Mom?" Emily replied nervously.

Emily's mom asked, "Did you finish the first part of your journal? We are almost ready to go to the park."

What was Emily going to do? She didn't do her work. She was going to ruin the vacation for everyone.

"I just finished Mom," Emily said panicked.

"Good, bring it in here and let me see it," her mom answered.

Oh, no! What was Emily going to do? She lied and now she was going to get caught. She may as well go tell her parents.

Emily went into the other room and told them that she forgot her journal at home, and then she lied so she didn't ruin everyone's vacation. While she was crying, she said she was sorry about one million times. Emily's parents told her to go sit down while they talked about her punishment for lying.

Emily's parents said that they were very disappointed in her for lying and even though they were on vacation there would be a punishment. They decided that they would be leaving one day early.

Emily was very upset, but she understood now what she did was wrong. She asked her parents for help. Her father looked at his video camera and said, "I have an idea."

The three of them spent the rest of the day walking around to the different historical sites and videotaped themselves explaining them and even acting like historical people from that time. In the end, Emily learned a lot and had a great time. Now that work was out of the way, it was time to hit the park.

ENDING YOUR STORY

Ending your story is critical on this part of the test. You have a very short amount of time but you must finish the story in order to maximize your score. This means that you must resolve the conflict, or solve the problem. Often you can end the story in a similar way to your opening. You can have the character speaking, thinking, or getting involved in an action. Sometimes, an author will write a circular ending. In this type of ending, the author revisits the lead. Remember, endings are important to the story! You want to have impact on the reader with your final words.

In our story about Emily, she has forgotten her journal, which she needs for her school assignment, at home. In order for Emily to go to the amusement park, she must first complete her assignment about historic Williamsburg. Unfortunately, this is impossible without the journal. Emily lies to her parents at first but later admits that she has not done her work. Emily's parents are angry, and Emily cries. She asks them to help her solve this problem. Together, Emily and her parents decide to make a video journal of their trip. They have fun performing and describing the historic sites. At the end, Emily makes it to the amusement park and rides the roller coaster she had been waiting for.

How can we write an exciting closing for this story? Let's look at a few examples. The first idea would be to end with an action, such as Emily riding down the roller coaster.

Emily's long hair flew behind her as she catapulted down the huge hill of Mountain Adventure. She could barely contain the excitement as she threw her arms in the air and let out a loud scream. Her smile stretched across her entire face as she thought to herself, I sure am lucky to be here. Then it slowly started to disappear, as she realized she could have been at the park for an extra day if she had just been honest with her parents from the start.

A circular ending might work if we revisit the scene of Emily with her suitcase. Reread the opening from earlier:

Emily frantically dumped her suitcase out. She threw her new pink bathing suit across the room followed by her yellow sundress and the matching flip-flops. She tore through each piece of clothes before burying her face into the pillow of the hotel bed. Tears poured out of her brown eyes. "Forgetting that journal is going to ruin my vacation," Emily mumbled to herself.

Now, let's try an ending:

Emily slowly folded her clothes and put them back into the suitcase. First her new pink bathing suit, which wasn't so new anymore. Then the yellow sundress and matching flip-flops. She thought back to the fun she had with her parents as they acted like the Colonists of Williamsburg and of the excitement of Mountain Adventure. "Forgetting that journal didn't ruin my vacation," Emily said to herself as she proudly held her videotape journal. "It just slowed me down a little."

PRACTICE ENDING YOUR STORY

It's your turn! Look back at your story plan. How might you end the story? Will you make Emily involved in an action? Maybe, you'll use dialogue or have Emily thinking. Perhaps, you'll even try a circular ending!

I will end with: _____ the character speaking
_____ the character thinking
_____ the character in action
_____ a circular ending

_____

_____

_____

_____

_____

_____

_____

_____

_____

_____

_____

_____

_____

_____

_____

_____

_____

_____

Now it is your turn to practice! On the following pages, you will find two sample writing prompts. Space is left after each prompt to draw and fill in your own pie chart. You then have three or four blank pages to write your story. Make sure you read the directions carefully. You only have 30 minutes for this writing task. It is very important that you set a timer for yourself or ask someone to set the time for you and have them tell you when to start and when time is up. Good Luck! Remember to use all of the hints you have learned so far.

Hints for Success

■ Prewrite! Prewrite! Prewrite!—Planning your idea for a story will not only give a place to begin, it will also show you how to finish. You only have 30 minutes for this part of the test. When you do not prewrite, you will spend precious minutes trying to figure out where to go next.

■ Start Strong!—Choose one of the four ways to begin your story: the character thinking, the character in action, the character speaking, or a vivid description. Be clear and specific. Use your best vocabulary.

■ Stay on topic!—With only 30 minutes to write, make sure you stay with the problem of your story at all times. If Emily cannot find her journal, do not spend time telling the reader what souvenirs she wants to buy.

■ Finish Stronger!—Choose one of the four ways to end your story: the character thinking, the character in action, the character speaking, or a circular ending. Vivid descriptions and a clear resolution to the main character's problem will pack your story with a powerful punch.

When you finish writing the first prompt, read the sample story that follows at the end of the book. This is a sample story that would receive a high score on the NJ ASK5. Also, read and use the rubric on page 44 so you can decide how your story would be scored. The rubric is what someone will use when they grade your story. The person will read your essay and decide if you are a strong writer, a writer who is good but makes some mistakes, or a writer who needs more practice to create a good story. Remember you only have 30 minutes for each one. Plan your ideas, use your skills, and do your best! Good luck!

PRACTICE TIME!

You will have 30 minutes to complete the following task. You may want to use the first 5 minutes to plan out your ideas. Make sure you leave enough time to revise and edit your work. Keep the writing hints in mind as you work.

PRACTICE

Sample Prompt #1

Steven was walking to his friend's house when he found a wallet on the side of the road. The identification was missing, but a large sum of money was inside it. Steven shows it to his friend who tells him to keep it. Steven does not know what to do. Write a story about Steven and how he decides what he should do with the wallet.

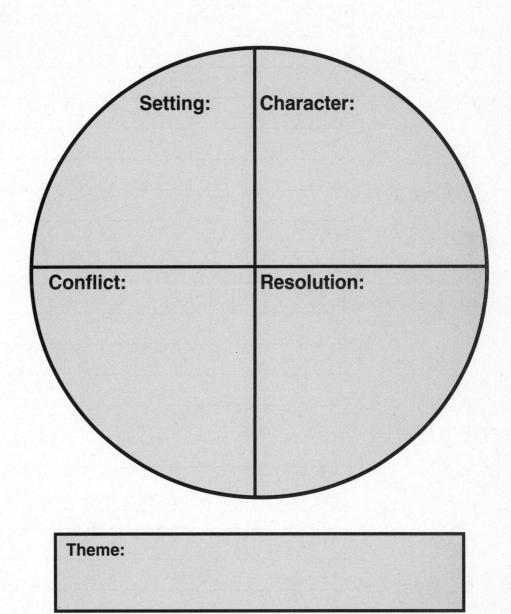

Setting:

Character:

Conflict:

Resolution:

Theme:

_____

_____

_____

_____

_____

_____

_____

_____

_____

_____

_____

_____

_____

_____

_____

_____

_____

_____

_____

(Answers on pp. 167–170.)

PRACTICE

Sample Prompt #2

> When Alex arrives home from school, his parents are waiting for him. His father tells him to get cleaned up and come back; they want to talk to him about a surprise. Alex is nervous. What could the surprise be? Write a story about Alex and what his parents tell him.

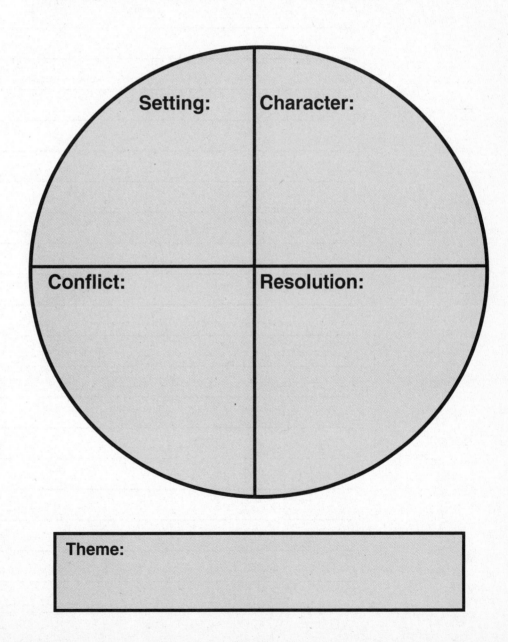

Setting:

Character:

Conflict:

Resolution:

Theme:

(Answers on pp. 170–173.)

EXPLANATORY WRITING

WHAT IS EXPLANATORY WRITING?

Can you see a word inside "explanatory"? If you said "explain" or "explanation," good job! That should tell you exactly what explanatory writing is. Explanatory writing is asking you to write an essay or composition that explains what you think. If you did well with speculative writing, you will also be good at explanatory writing. Speculative writing asks you to guess, or speculate, about what might happen in a story. Explanatory writing will ask you to explain what you think about a topic or situation. It also may require you to read something and then explain your opinion. If this sounds like a lot, do not worry. Use what you know about speculative writing, add in a different way to prewrite, and you will be an explanatory writing expert before you know it!

IT'S ALL IN THE DETAILS!

It is true. The details that you add to your writing are going to make you successful in explanatory writing.

When a friend tells you a story, which ones do you like best? The ones with enough detail so you can understand what happened, right? Without enough details, you have too many questions. With too many details, you may get bored. So we need to make sure that we have a way to plan our short essay so we can remember to add all of the necessary details.

With this composition or essay, like the speculative prompt, you will have only 30 minutes. It is very important that you spend your time working smartly so you do not run out of time. We recommend that you spend the first 5 minutes thinking of your idea and prewriting, 20 minutes writing, and the last 5 minutes revising and editing. You will be given 30 minutes. It is important that you use all the time you are given. You do not earn extra points by being done early. All right, let's get going. Read the sample prompt below.

Sample Prompt

Your parents have told you that you can choose any room in the house to redesign. They are allowing you to make all of the decisions. In a well-written composition, explain what room in your house you would change. Make sure you explain why you chose that room and what changes you would make.

Okay, now that you read the prompt, you have to make sure you know what to do. What do you have to write? What information do they want you to include? Do you think you have those answers? Great! Let's think about prewriting.

PREWRITING

For this type of writing, we are going to use a web to prewrite. Can you picture a web? It has a center and all the strings come from the center, right? That is how our web is going to work. Our main idea will be in the center and all of the details will be put into the parts surrounding our main idea. So the center of our web will be the room that we choose to write about. On the line below, write the name of the room you would choose.

Good. For our example, we are going to choose the family room. In the center of our web are the words "family room." That will be our first paragraph, our introduction. Next we need to explain why we chose this room. So you do not get confused, think of your web as a clock. Write the notes about your first body paragraph at 12:00, your second at 3:00, your third at 6:00, and your conclusion at 9:00. This will be clearer as we finish our prewriting. When finished, you will have four or five short paragraphs that need to be completed in 30 minutes. An example of the web is shown below.

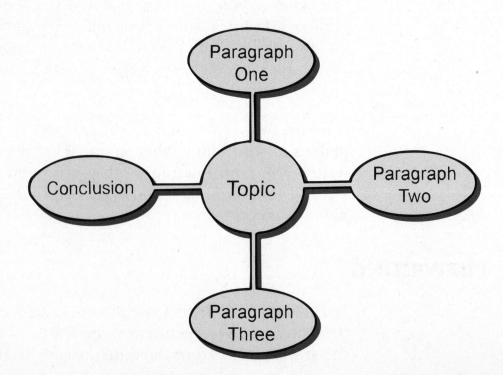

Now, we selected the family room as the room to redesign. In our first paragraph we will write about the room, describing the room and what we would do to it. The second paragraph will begin to explain why the room is important. If you think of any details, you can extend the detail from your main point. The third paragraph will be one way we will redesign the room. The fourth paragraph will be another change to the room, and the fifth paragraph will be our conclusion. Remember, the idea of an explanatory essay is for the writer to explain his or her thoughts clearly. If you create a graphic organizer and fill it in completely, you will have all of the information you will need to write an excellent explanatory essay. Here is an example of what your prewriting may look like.

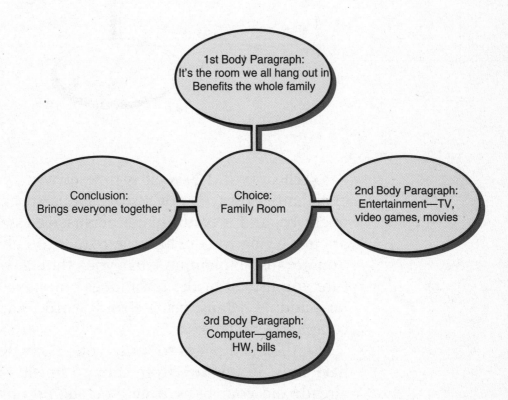

Now that you see how your prewriting can look, are you ready to try your own? Good. A web has been drawn for you below. Remember, you do not have to use all of the blank spaces or you can add more if you need them.

When you are done, check over your web to see if you added enough reasons to support your choice. Then it will be time to write.

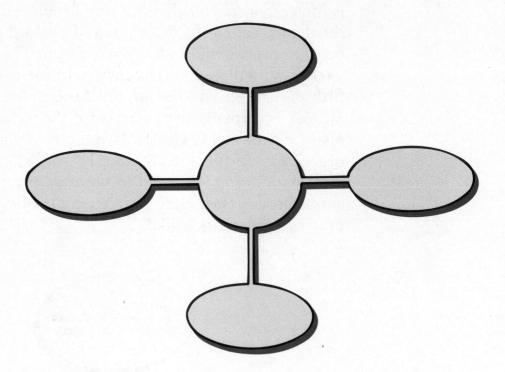

Excellent work! Now it is time to write your essay. The explanatory essay is not a story like a speculative essay might be, and it is not like a persuasive essay because you are not trying to convince the reader to believe your side. You are just explaining what your thoughts are. So make sure you use all of the techniques you have practiced so far—adding details, using strong words, and writing complete sentences.

Use the lined pages to write your essay. Remember, you have only 30 minutes from start to finish. Since you already did your prewriting, you should only write for 20 minutes and use 5 minutes to revise and edit. An example essay is provided for you to compare your essay.

How did you do? Great. Here is an example essay for this topic. Compare yours to the example and use the rubric on page 44 to score your essay.

Sample Essay

The news that my family was going to remodel one of the rooms in my house was so exciting. It was even more exciting when I found out that I get to pick the room that the family is going to change. That is a big decision. If my family were to remodel one room in the house, I would choose the family room.

The family room would be the best room to remodel. This is because it is the place where we spend most of our free time. Remodeling the family room benefits the whole family. It will give us a chance to spend more time together and make great memories.

There are so many changes I would make to the family room. It isn't very big, but the first thing we would do is paint it blue, my favorite color. Then we would go buy a new

50 inch plasma hdtv, a new video game system, and some movies to watch. This would give the family something to do together.

Next, our family would need a place to put our computer system. On our new computer desk, I would put a brand new computer with room to store all of my family's favorite songs so we could enjoy our music together and maybe dance. I could also use the computer for my homework, and my mom and dad would also use it to pay their bills.

Designing a new room would be hard work, but it would also be a lot of fun. My family would have to work hard to create a room everyone would enjoy. If I could pick any room in my house to change, I would pick my family room. Now my family has a place that they never want to leave.

PRACTICE

Explanatory Writing

Now is your chance to practice another explanatory essay. Remember, you have 30 minutes. Prewrite for 5 minutes. Write for 20 minutes. Revise and edit for five minutes. Set a timer or have someone tell you when to begin and end. Good luck.

> Your parents insist that you clean out your room and sell some of your seldom-used items at the family yard sale. Choose one item from your room that you refuse to sell and explain why you would keep that item.

_____

_____

_____

_____

_____

_____

_____

_____

_____

_____

_____

_____

_____

_____

_____

_____

_____

_____

_____

_____

_____

_____

_____

_____

_____

_____

_____

_____

_____

_____

_____

_____

_____

_____

_____

_____

(Answers on pp. 173–175.)

Chapter 6

DON'T GET CAUGHT . . .

This chapter will help you avoid making common errors when writing your composition, story, or open-ended responses. This might be review or new information for you. Either way, take some time to make sure these mistakes don't catch you.

SENTENCE STRUCTURE

To be a successful writer, you need to understand sentence structure. This is important because you will want to vary the types of sentences you use in order to create an interesting piece of writing. Let's start by identifying what forms a complete sentence. There are two parts to every sentence: the subject and the predicate. The subject is who or what the sentence is about, and the predicate is the action of the sentence.

> Subject = Noun (person, place, thing)
> Predicate = Verb (action, state of being)

Read the sentence below and identify the subject and the predicate.

The dog ran.

The subject is *The dog* because the sentence is about the dog. *Ran* is the predicate because this is the action of the dog. Note that "dog" is the noun and "ran" is the verb.

A common mistake is to write only a subject or only a predicate. If this happens, the author does not have a complete sentence, but instead has a fragment. Look at the samples below.

The excited dog.

This is not a complete sentence because it only includes a subject. The readers know the sentence is about an excited dog but doesn't know the action of the dog because the predicate is missing.

Ran through the field.

This is not a complete sentence. The readers know that someone or something ran through the field, but they don't know who is doing this action. In this case the subject is missing.

PRACTICE

Writing Complete Sentences

Each sentence fragment below is missing either the subject or predicate. Fix each and then check your answers in the back of the book.

1. The lonely boy.

_____

_____

2. The angry teacher.

_____

_____

3. Played video games for hours.

_____

_____

4. Announced he won the lottery.

_____

_____

(Answers on pp. 176–177.)

Now, why is it important to understand subject and predicate? There are several different types of sentences. To write them correctly, you'll need to understand the independent clause. An independent clause consists of a subject and a predicate. It can stand alone or be part of a sentence. By this definition

The dog ran.

is an independent clause. On the other hand, a dependent clause has a subject and predicate but cannot stand alone. It doesn't make sense unless it is attached to an independent clause.

Independent Clause (IC) = subject and predicate and can stand alone
Dependent Clause (DC) = subject and predicate but cannot stand alone

Look at the example below.

The happy dog greeted his owner.

This is an independent clause because it has a subject and a predicate and can stand alone.

When the happy dog saw his owner.

This is a dependent clause. It has a subject and predicate but cannot stand alone. It is an incomplete thought. What did the dog do when he saw his owner? For this clause to make sense, it needs to be attached to an independent clause.

When the happy dog saw his owner, he wagged his tail.

Once the independent clause, "he wagged his tail," is added, the sentence makes sense and is complete.

A common error when writing sentences is to combine two independent clauses using only a comma. This is called a **comma splice** and can be fixed by making the two independent clauses separate sentences or by adding a conjunction such as *and, but,* or *so.* Another solution is to make one independent clause into a dependent clause.

A second common error is to combine two independent clauses without any punctuation. This is called a **run-on sentence**. This mistake can also be fixed by separating the independent clauses into two sentences or by adding a comma and conjunction. Again, the author could make one independent clause a dependent clause. Take a look at the examples that follow.

> Comma splice = combining two independent clauses with only a comma
> Run-on sentence = combining two independent clauses with no punctuation

Comma splice:

The dog barked, he scared the little girl.

Run-on sentence:

The dog barked he scared the little girl.

Fix-it technique 1: Form two sentences

The dog barked. He scared the little girl.

Fix-it technique 2: Combine the two independent clauses with a conjunction

The dog barked, and he scared the little girl.

Fix-it technique 3: Change one independent clause into a dependent clause

When the dog barked, he scared the little girl.

In the third fix-it technique the author made "The dog barked" into the dependent clause "When the dog barked." This is a dependent clause because it has a subject *dog* and an action or predicate *barked*, but it cannot stand alone. By itself, the clause does not make sense. This type of strategy is the most sophisticated fix-it technique of the three. When practicing, try to apply this technique.

PRACTICE

Sentence Structure

Fix each comma splice or run-on sentence. Try to use each fix-it technique at least once. Then, check your answers in the back of the book.

1. Tyler dove for the ball, he made the third out.

_____

_____

2. Josie performed in the talent show she won first place.

_____

_____

3. My cat cuddled on the couch, he purred when I pet him.

_____

_____

4. Reed studied for her science test she aced it.

_____

_____

(Answers on p. 177.)

Successful authors vary the sentence structure in their writing. We're going to focus on three types of sentence structures. The first is called a simple sentence. A **simple sentence** consists of one independent clause. The second type of sentence is called a **compound sentence** and is formed with two independent clauses. The third is a **complex sentence**. This is a more sophisticated sentence to write because it consists of one independent clause and one or more dependent clauses.

> Simple sentence = 1 independent clause
> Compound sentence = 2 independent clauses
> Complex sentence = 1 independent clause and 1 or more dependent clauses

Read the examples below.

Simple sentence:

The playful puppy chased the ball.

Compound sentence:

> The playful puppy chased the ball, and then he napped on the couch.

Complex sentence:

> After the playful puppy chased the ball, he napped on the couch.

PRACTICE

Sentence Variety

It's your turn to try to write each type of sentence. Use the space below to write three sentences about your favorite hobby.

1. Simple Sentence

_____

_____

2. Compound Sentence

_____

_____

3. Complex Sentence

_____

_____

(Answers on p. 178.)

HOMOPHONE MIX-UPS

One of the most common mistakes young authors make is the misuse of homophones. A **homophone** is defined as one of two or more words that sound alike but have different meanings. For example, *ate* and *eight* sound alike but one means to consume food and the other defines a number. As you write you need to be careful that you are using the right homonym. Review the following list of common homophones.

There	(Adverb) At or in that place Please wait over there.
They're	Contraction of *they are* They're going for ice-cream after the game.
Their	(Possessive adjective) Belonging to them Sydney and Olivia put the books in their lockers.
To	(Preposition) Toward She went to the teacher and asked for extra help.
Too	(Adverb) Also; more than enough I have too many stuffed animals to fit in my room.
Two	Number He bought two bags of chips in the cafeteria.
Allowed	(Past tense verb) To allow or permit Avery's parents allowed her to attend the slumber party.
Aloud	(Adverb) Vocally; with a loud voice My dad reads aloud to me before bed.

Effect Affect	(Noun) Result or consequence of something The effect of studying was earning an A on the test. (Verb) To change or influence someone or something Mrs. Simpson, my fourth grade teacher, affected my life because she taught me to believe in myself.
Threw Through	(Past tense verb) To throw The quarterback threw the ball for a touchdown. (Preposition) Passing from one place to another The player kicked the ball through the goal post.
Weather Whether	(Noun) State of the atmosphere in regards to temperature, precipitation, etc. The weather was cold and rainy. (Conjunction) Used to indicate a single alternative I need to decide whether to buy a Honda or a Toyota.
Plain Plane	(Adjective) Not fancy Janet likes plain food rather than spicy food. (Noun) Shortened version of airplane The plane departed for Florida early this morning
Where Wear	(Adverb) In what position or circumstance Where is the remote control? (Verb) To be dressed in I decided to wear my green sweater today.
No Know	(Adverb) To express refusal No! I will not let you copy my homework. (Verb) To have knowledge Christofer didn't know where he left his sneakers.

Here	(Adverb) At this place
	Is your homework here or at home?
Hear	(Verb) To listen
	Did you hear the new song by Beyonce?
Then	(Adverb) Next in order of time or place
	We went to the movies and then we ate pizza.
Than	(Conjunction) Used in making a comparison
	My sister is taller than me.

PRACTICE

Homophones

Choose the correct word for each sentence. Then check your answers in the back of the book.

1. The brothers spent hours playing _____ video games. (there / their / they're)

2. Molly ordered a _____ donut rather than one with sprinkles. (plane / plain)

3. Jayme looked _____ his binder for the homework. (threw / through)

4. I don't know _____ I should go for a run or a hike. (whether / weather)

5. The _____ of the fire was devastating. (effect / affect)

6. Melissa has _____ many pairs of shoes. (to / too / two)

7. My parents _____ the decisions I make. (effect / affect)

8. The teacher asked Michele to read the paragraph _____. (allowed / aloud)

9. Listen closely and you will _____ the sounds of crickets. (here / hear)

10. I like math better _____ science. (then / than)

(Answers on pp. 178–179.)

WRITING INTERESTING DIALOGUE

When people talk, it is called dialogue. Dialogue can make a story more exciting if it is done well, but it can be tricky. There are lots of rules for dialogue and hints to make it interesting. When writing dialogue you are going to use quotation marks around words the character is speaking. You will also sometimes include a tag to tell the reader which character is talking.

Let's first look at punctuating dialogue. Review the rules of dialogue and read the examples. Then, you will have a chance to practice.

PUNCTUATING DIALOGUE

When the tag is in front of the quotation,

■ Use a comma before the quotation mark

■ Capitalize the first word within the quotation marks

■ Include end punctuation inside the quotation marks

For example:

>   Mr. Riccardi exclaimed, "Fifth graders are awesome!"

When the tag is behind the quotation,

- Capitalize the first letter of the quotation
- Use a comma, question mark, or exclamation point before the tag but inside the quotation marks
- Use a period at the end of the sentence

For example:

>   "What is the hypothesis?" Ms. Magliato asked.
>
>   "Please take out your math homework," Ms. Blayne instructed.
>
>   "We won the game!" Coach Scire exclaimed.

When the tag interrupts the sentence,

- Capitalize the first letter of the sentence
- Use a comma inside the quotation before the tag and outside the quotation after the tag
- Do not capitalize the second half of the quote, unless it is a proper noun
- Include end punctuation inside the quotation marks

For example:

>   "This story," Mrs. Perillo said, "is one of my favorites."
>
>   "We will board the bus at 9:15," Mrs. Fava said, "and arrive at the museum around 10:00."

Warning
These rules apply **only** if a sentence is interrupted. Make sure the sentences are not independent. Independent sentences will include end punctuation after the tag and begin with a capital letter.

For example:

"We will meet by the entrance at 3:00," Mr. DeMarco instructed. "Once everyone is present we will walk back to the buses."

PRACTICE

Dialogue

Rewrite the following sentences using the rules of dialogue. Don't forget to check your capitalization. Then, check your answers in the back of the book.

1. who handed in permission slips Mrs. Jones asked

_____

_____

2. nick said I'll be in my room if you need me

_____

_____

3. on Tuesday you can come bowling said Samantha if you like soccer, you should come to the park on Saturday

_____

_____

4. today we will practice passing Coach Magnotti said

_____

_____

5. we will begin the experiment by gathering our materials Ms. Kaufhold directed and then we will dissect the worm

_____

_____

(Answers on p. 179.)

Writing good dialogue does not end at punctuation and capitalization. In order for dialogue to be effective, it needs to be surrounded by good narration. Narration is the story. Dialogue without narration is boring. Read the example below.

"What's wrong?" Rob asked Mason.

"Nothing," Mason answered.

"I know something is bothering you," Rob responded. "Just spill it."

"I'm failing math and Mom and Dad are going to kill me," Mason replied.

"I can help you," Rob said. "I'll tutor you after school."

Now, read the same dialogue with narration. Pay attention to how the writing has changed and improved because of the words surrounding the dialogue.

Mason sat on his bedroom floor with his head in his hands. The door creaked open and his older brother Rob poked his head through the door. "What's wrong? Rob asked.

"Nothing," Mason answered staring down at the floor, trying to hold in the tears.

"I know something is bothering you," Rob responded as he sat next to his little brother. "Just spill it." Rob lovingly put his arm around Mason who was four years younger.

"I'm failing math and Mom and Dad are going to kill me," Mason finally replied with a look of desperation.

"I can help you," Rob said. "I'll tutor you after school." A look of relief came across Mason's face. Maybe Mom and Dad wouldn't be so mad if Rob was going to help him.

With narration, the reader learns more about the characters and plot. This is more interesting dialogue than the previous passage.

PRACTICE

Writing Dialogue

Read the boring dialogue. Then rewrite it with narration to make it more interesting for the reader.

"Come on Leo. No one's going to find out," Harley said.

"I don't know," Leo replied.

"I'm sure Ryan will let me copy. He's a good friend," Harley said.

"It's just that I studied really hard and I don't want to lose points if we get caught," Leo said.

"Trust me, we won't get caught," Harley replied.

"Maybe you should ask Ryan," Leo said.

_____

_____

_____

_____

_____

_____

(Answers on pp. 179–180.)

USING I AND ME

It is easy to confuse or misuse I and me when writing or speaking, but there is an easy fix to the problem. "I" is a pronoun and must be the subject of a sentence. "Me" is a pronoun that must be used as the object of a sentence. This means it will receive the action of the verb. Read the examples below.

I = pronoun used as a subject

I am going to the mall.

Kelly and I are going to the mall.

Me = pronoun used as an object

Kelly is going to the mall with me.

Kelly is going to the mall with Rachel and me.

Often when the author writes a sentence with more than one subject or more than one object, it is confusing whether he or she should write "I" or "me." There is an easy test to figure out the correct use. Simply remove the other noun from the sentence and decide if it makes sense. Look at the examples below.

John and me went to the dance on Friday.

Remove the other noun, "John," and see if it makes sense.

Me went to the dance on Friday. (Does not make sense!)

I went to the dance on Friday. (Makes sense!)

Based on the test, we can figure out the sentence should read,

John and I went to the dance.

Furthermore, "I" is part of the subject; therefore, we know it is correct. Let's look at one more example, and then you will practice.

Sophie came with Jessie and I to the amusement park.

Remove the other noun, "Jessie," and see if it makes sense.

Sophie came with I to the amusement park. (Does not make sense!)

Sophie came with me to the amusement park. (Makes sense!)

The sentence should read:

Sophie came with Jessie and me to the amusement park.

In this sentence "me" is the object not the subject. We know it is the object because it receives the action of the verb. In this sentence the action or verb is "came" and "Sophie" is the subject. Who came? Sophie. Where did she come? With Jessie and me to the amusement park.

PRACTICE

I and Me

Complete each sentence with either "I" or "me" and then check your answers in the back of the book.

1. Mia, Hannah, Rhea, and _____ will be a group for the project.

2. Toby and _____ went to the library to study for the science exam.

3. Would you like to hang out with Sam, Nicole, and _____?

4. Please, come to the dance with Dan and
_____.

5. Michele hit Grace and _____ home with
her triple.

(Answers on p. 180.)

ANSWERS TO PRACTICE QUESTIONS

CHAPTER 1
HINTS FOR SUCCESS (pp. 36–37)

1. **C.** The transition "first of all" can only be used to start the first paragraph of the body of the essay. "For example" and "However" are transitions in the middle of the paragraph and "Finally" is for your last body paragraph.

2. **A.** "Hysterical" is a synonym for funny. "Cute" could be used when writing funny, but it is not the best way. You should have been able to cross out "horrible" and "depressing" since neither word means funny.

3. **D.** To have a complete sentence, you need to have a subject, verb, and complete thought. Both A and C have all three of those. Choice B ("Ran quickly down the street") does not have a subject, so the sentence is not complete.

4. **A.** The last three are all transitions you would use in the beginning of a paragraph. "For example" is used in the middle of the paragraph when you are trying to prove a reason.

5. **A.** "Horrible" is the best word you can choose. "Bad" could be a choice, but it is not the *best* word. "Worse" and "lonely" do not make sense in the sentence.

6. **D.** It is a run-on sentence. For D to be a complete sentence, add the word "and" before the third "I." The sentence would read, "I slipped on the ice, I bruised my knee, and I bumped my head."

SAMPLE ESSAY AND EXPLANATION (p. 39)

Imagine this scene in a park in this town. It is Saturday afternoon. The sun is shining, and the sounds of children laughing, cheering, and celebrating fill the air. A strange sound is mixed in with the voices, and you cannot quite place it. The noise is a constant clicking over and over again. Then there is a low thump, followed by cheers. Walking over to the noise, you realize that the clicking is skateboard wheels rolling over the pavement, and the cheering is for children performing different skate tricks. This would be a common Saturday afternoon if our town had a skate park. Our town is considering different activities for their after-school recreation program. Building a skate park is a great idea because skateboarding encourages sportsmanship, provides exercise, and is a growing sport.

First of all, skateboarding is one of the fastest growing sports in America. It seems like a new friend starts skating every day. If you go outside your house right now, you will probably see a skateboarder before you see a child playing any other sport. In addition to this, skateboarding is all over television. Every year there are competitions on TV that a lot of people watch. Skateboarders from all over the world compete for medals just like in the Olympics.

Next, skateboarding promotes good sportsmanship. In some sports, competition is very important, but sometimes it is taken too far. Teams do not like each other. In skateboarding, good sportsmanship happens naturally. Everyone is encouraged to try a new trick and everyone cheers when the skater is successful. Skaters want each other to get better and will help each other. What other sport does that?

Most importantly, skateboarding is great exercise. All of the movements on a skateboard come from your feet and legs. You have to push on the ground with one foot while you stay balanced on your board. If you want to do any tricks, you have to have a strong upper body to hold your board or even hold your body up. Your lungs get exercise while you are skating around. It is a great way to stay in shape.

In conclusion, a skate park would be a great idea for an after-school activity in our town. Children would learn good sportsmanship, get exercise, and participate in a growing sport. Our town would be the envy of every other town if we had our own skate park. Help make that happen and build a skate park.

Explanation

This essay has all of the basics needed in a persuasive essay. It has a strong thesis, three specific reasons, and supporting details. The essay also provides examples for each reason. There was obviously planning done before the essay was written because the support was specific. The introduction started with a strong interest catcher to put a picture in the reader's mind. The conclusion repeated the important parts to remind the reader what to remember.

How did you do on your essay? Use this essay as an example and check the rubric provided in the book to see how you did. You will have more opportunities to write a persuasive essay on the sample tests at the end of the book.

CHAPTER 2

CONTEXT CLUES (pp. 51–52)

1. Clues: A lion pounces. I think a lion pounces to catch or attack other animals for food. Mom is going to pounce because she is angry.

   Definition: Pounce sounds like it would be a sudden attack.

2. Clues: The paper was jabbing back and forth, so it sounds like it is moving in some way. Mom looked like a knight trying to slay the evil dragon. A knight would use a sword to do this and would wave it around.

   Definition: Jabbed must mean that mom quickly stabbed or thrust the paper forward toward Connor like a knife or sword.

THE PLOT (pp. 55–56)

Exposition: Connor is coming home from elementary school to a very angry mom.

Rising action: Mom confronts Connor about the letter from school. Connor had already erased phone messages from the teacher and principal. Then, he lies about shooting spitballs and blames his best friend Robbie. Connor's mom calls Robbie's mom to straighten things out.

Climax or turning point: Connor interrupts his mom's phone call to admit the truth.

Falling action: Connor realizes his mom wasn't really talking to Robbie's mom. He is sent to his room.

Resolution: Connor will be punished, and he thinks it will be a biggie.

THE THEME (p. 57)

Possible answers for theme are:

- Honesty is the best policy.
- Treat others the way you want to be treated.
- Don't lie to your mom.

The Look—MULTIPLE-CHOICE QUESTIONS (pp. 61–62)

1. **B.** If pounce means ready to attack then she must be angry.

2. **C.** Connor has lied multiple times in the story and erased phone messages so his mom wouldn't hear them. This indicates that he is dishonest and sneaky.

3. **D.** Connor realizes he will be punished for his actions.

4. **D.** He was hiding it from his mom. We know that mom had not gotten the messages based on her reaction to the letter from school.

5. **B.** The author is comparing the lies to lava flowing without using the word "like" or "as." If the author had used either of these two words, this would be a simile rather than a metaphor.

The Look—OPEN-ENDED QUESTION (p. 65)

Check your own answer to see if you included each of the following parts. Then, read the sample answer below.

I restated the question? _____

I used evidence from the text? _____

I made a personal connection? _____

I have a concluding sentence? _____

Sample Open-Ended Response

It was fair for Connor's mom to trick him into telling her the truth. She probably found out about the phone calls in the letter from the school so she knew he was being dishonest. Since Connor erased the messages, she probably believed what was in the letter rather than his lies. If Connor wasn't being honest, then she had the right to trick him into telling the truth. In the end, she found out he was lying again when he told her Robbie had shot the spitballs. Once I lied to my parents about breaking my mom's favorite vase. When she found out I was in bigger trouble for the lie than I would have been in for just breaking the vase. Connor will probably have a similar situation. He'll be in more trouble now than he would have been for shooting the spitballs in the first place. Hopefully Connor will learn his lesson about lying to his mom.

NARRATIVE TEXT (pp. 71–74)

A Night to Remember—Multiple-Choice Questions

1. A. Abby is really listening and paying attention, hoping to hear someone coming to rescue her.

2. C. Abby's heart skipped a beat, she jumps up and is smiling. She definitely thinks someone is coming to find her.

3. **D.** In the text it states that the girls need fire to cook and stay warm.

4. **D.** Mrs. Watts instructs the girls to stay with a friend and don't wander too far.

5. **D.** Abby thinks the rocks are a good place to hang out.

6. **B.** Abby gathers branches and leaves in order to provide protection from the cold.

7. **C.** Abby saw the flashlights and began yelling for help.

8. **C.** Mrs. Watts says she's happy Abby is okay but has a scowl on her face. She must have been upset that Abby didn't follow her directions.

9. **A.** Statues stay frozen in one place. At this part of the story, Abby wasn't moving because she was frightened and didn't want to draw attention to herself.

10. **D.** Abby realizes that she should have been working like the other girls and following directions. She proves this by doing the dishes at the end of the story.

A Night to Remember—Open-Ended Question

11. Check your own answer to see if you included each of the following parts. Then, read the sample answer below.

_____ I restated the question?

_____ I used evidence from the text?

_____ I made a personal connection?

_____ I have a concluding sentence?

In the beginning of the story, Abby thinks that camping should be an easy vacation. She doesn't want to help around camp by pitching the tent or gathering wood for the fire. When her scout leader gives directions, Abby doesn't take them seriously and wanders off by herself. After being lost and scared, Abby realizes that camping takes some work and that she should have followed directions. This is evident because Abby apologizes for her actions and helps out at camp by doing the dishes. The first time I went camping I didn't think it would be such hard work either. Like Abby, I expected it to be all fun and no work. Since then I have learned to love camping. Hopefully Abby will give camping a second chance after learning from this experience.

CHAPTER 3

INDENTIFYING THE THESIS STATEMENT (pp. 81–82)

Paragraph 1: As you decide the best pet for you and your family, you will need to weigh the positives and negatives of owning either a dog or a cat.

Paragraph 2: In this paragraph the thesis statement is implied, which means the author doesn't come right out and tell the reader. Instead, the reader needs to figure out what the article will be about. A possible thesis statement is the following: Teens should not smoke because it is dangerous to their health.

SCHOOL LUNCHES: ARE THEY HEALTHY?—MULTIPLE-CHOICE QUESTIONS (pp. 85–86)

1. **C.** The article talks about why cafeteria regulations need to be examined and offers both sides of the argument.

2. **D.** In this sentence it appears that the government is making rules or requirements for school cafeteria foods.

3. **B.** The author tells the reader this information.

4. **A.** According to the text, kids choose to eat the snacks instead.

5. **B.** More than 9 million kids today are overweight or obese.

6. **D.** Obesity causes a greater risk for heart disease, diabetes, and cancer.

SCHOOL LUNCHES: ARE THEY HEALTHY?—OPEN-ENDED QUESTION (p. 89)

Check your own answer to see if you included each of the following parts. Then, read the sample answer below.

_____ I restated the question?

_____ I used evidence from the text?

_____ I made a personal connection?

_____ I have a concluding sentence?

Even with state regulations, school lunches are still not healthy for kids. This is mainly because a large number of kids choose not to eat the complete lunch and instead splurge on bags of baked chips and packs of low-fat cookies. Although these are healthier alternatives, it is not nutritious for kids to eat only junk food for lunch. At my school, very few kids eat the lunch planned to hit all five food groups, and if children aren't going to eat this, then what is the point of state regulations? For this reason, New Jersey should abandon food regulations in school cafeterias.

EXPOSITORY TEXT (pp. 94–96)

Video Games: Helping or Hurting Kids Today—Multiple-Choice Questions

1. **D.** This information is clearly stated in the opening paragraph.

2. **B.** Parents are concerned because children spend too much time in front of the television.

3. **A.** The article defines aggressive behavior as hitting, kicking, and fighting. These acts would be unfriendly and deliberate, not accidental.

4. **D.** The article states that kids who play violent video games are more aggressive and that younger children are more influenced by games than older children.

5. **D.** The article defines aggression through these behaviors.

6. **C.** The author clearly states this in the fourth paragraph.

7. **C.** Logic and problem solving, exercise, and hand-eye coordination are all benefits of playing video games.

8. **A.** The reader needs to draw the conclusion that the games are helping the child develop thinking skills that benefit them in school.

9. **D.** Although the article does talk about video games being harmful to kids, the entire article is not about this. The article is about the advantages and disadvantages of gaming.

Video Games: Helping or Hurting Kids Today— Open-Ended Question

10. Check your own answer to see if you included each of the following parts. Then, read the sample answer below.

_____ I restated the question?

_____ I used evidence from the text?

_____ I made a personal connection?

_____ I have a concluding sentence?

Children do not spend too much time playing video games. Thirteen hours for an entire week is not very much considering there are 168 hours in a week. In addition, the time spent playing is actually helping kids. Not only are they using their brains for thinking and problem solving, but they are also learning to follow directions and eye–hand coordination. I have a Nintendo Wii, so when I play games I am also getting exercise. All of the benefits of playing video games are more important than the few disadvantages.

CHAPTER 4

SAMPLE PROMPT #1 (p. 114)

I can't believe my bike has a flat tire, Steven thought to himself as he walked to his best friend Joe's house. Walking wasn't a big deal and Jay's house was right around the corner, but Steven loved his bike. He took it everywhere.

Just as Steven was about to turn the corner to Joe's street, something on the edge of the street caught his eye. A wallet! Steven looked around and then picked it up. He looked inside. It was empty except for $200! A wallet with no I.D. and $200. Steven practically flew the rest of the way to Joe's house.

"Guess what!" Steven pushed past Joe as the door opened.

"Hey, watch it! I don't know—what?" Joe answered as he stumbled out of the way.

Steven's hands pushed his red hair out of his eyes. "You're not going to believe what I found." Steven held up the wallet.

"Yeah, so you have a wallet. I have one too," Joe said.

"Not one you found on the side of the road. One with $200 in it!" Joe screamed.

"Are you kidding?" Joe snatched the wallet. "Wow—no I.D. That means it's all yours. You're rich!"

Steven had not thought about keeping it or not. He was so excited, he had not really thought it through. He couldn't keep it, could he?

"I can't keep it," Steven said.

"Of course you can," Joe shot back, "No I.D. remember?"

All of that money would be great. With $200, Steven would have enough money for the new bike he was saving for plus a couple of games for his Nintendo Wii. No one would ever know.

"I can't," Steven answered, "It wouldn't be right. How would you feel if you lost this?"

"I wouldn't be stupid enough to lose $200, but I guess I would feel pretty bad," Joe sighed.

Steven thought about it again for a minute. Yes, he definitely had to give it back. It was the right thing to do. He asked to use Joe's phone.

"Hi Mom. Um, I found a wallet. Could you pick me up so I could drop it off at the police station?"

Explanation

What did the author do here to make this a good piece of writing? Let's think back to what we learned in this chapter. First off, how did the author begin the story? He started off with the character thinking and in the middle of an action. Steven thought about the flat tire as he walked his bike to his friend's house. The author introduced the problem in an interesting way by not letting the author know what Steven saw at first but then revealing it was a wallet with money but no identification.

The author added description to his story by **showing** the reader how Joe moved, he stumbled, and what Steven looked like, he pushed his red hair out of his eyes. The author also used good word choice and dialogue to make the story interesting.

Most importantly, the author **solved the problem.** When you write your story, you will need to make sure you have a problem and you solve the problem. In this story, Steven needed to make a tough decision. Should he keep the wallet or turn it in to the police? The story ended with dialogue, letting the reader know Steven's decision to drop the wallet off at the police station.

Take a look back at the story you wrote, and use the checklist below to help you evaluate your own writing.

▪ How did you start your story? I started with my character . . .

_____ thinking

_____ talking

_____ involved in an action

_____ or I wrote a descriptive scene

- ■ How about the middle of your story?

  _____ I had good word choice

  _____ I used show, don't tell details

- ■ How did you end the story?

  _____ I solved my problem

- ■ I ended with my character . . .

  _____ thinking

  _____ talking

  _____ involved in an action

  _____ or I created a circular ending

Keep this in mind as you try your next practice prompt. With a little more practice, you'll be writing great stories in no time!

SAMPLE PROMPT #2 (p. 119)

Wow, school was tough today, Alex thought as he lugged his backpack down the street to his house. Mrs. Smith piled on homework that would take Alex all night to finish. He would be chained to his chair from the time he walked in the door until bedtime. The only part that Alex was looking forward to was his essay. He had to write an essay about someplace he would like to visit. Alex always wanted to go to California, but his parents always said it was too much money.

As Alex turned into his driveway, he noticed his dad's car. Dad is never home this early, Alex thought. I hope everything is okay. Alex ran up the stairs to find out what was going on.

Walking into his house, Alex heard his parents talking in the other room.

"Hello?" Alex called.

"In here honey," Mom replied.

"Dad, what are you doing home early?"

"I have a surprise—so get cleaned up and come right back."

"Okay."

Alex turned and went into the bathroom down the hall. As he turned on the water to wash his hands, he wondered about the surprise. Would it be good or bad?

Dad always called bad things surprises. Like the time the family moved from Florida to New Jersey. That was bad at first, but now he liked it. What about all of the times that Dad thinks I won't like the food that was made for dinner? He always calls that a surprise too. Sometimes I do like the food that he makes.

Maybe this would not be so bad. Sometimes when Dad called something a surprise everything turned out good like Yankee tickets, baby brothers, and puppies. That was Alex's favorite surprise. Dad called from work to say he was coming home with a surprise. He showed up with Alex's best friend, Moose. He was a beagle with brown and white fur. He tried to act bigger than he really was so Alex called him Moose.

All right, it was time to go downstairs. This had to be like a band-aid. Rip it off quickly and it will not hurt for long. Alex left the bathroom and walked down the hall to see his parents. His palms were sweating, and he sat down quickly because he thought he was going to pass out.

"Okay Dad, I'm ready for the surprise," Alex mumbled.

"Boy you look nervous. I'd better get this over with quickly. How do you think Christmas in California sounds?"

Alex could not believe what he was hearing. His homework tonight was definitely going to be a lot easier.

Explanation

What did the author do here to make this a good piece of writing? Let's see if the author followed the hints for success. First, how did the author begin the story? He started off with the character thinking and in the middle of an action. Not only was Alex lugging his backpack home, but he was thinking about all his homework, especially his essay. When Alex got to his house, the author introduced the problem in an interesting way. Alex's Dad had a surprise, but Alex was nervous because his Dad's surprises were not always good.

Throughout the story, the author kept the reader anxious about the surprise. Would it be a good or bad outcome for Alex. The author added description to his story by showing the reader Alex was nervous, his palms were sweaty. In addition, the author also used good word choice and dialogue to make the story interesting.

Most importantly, the author solved the problem. Remember, you will need to make sure you solve the problem in your story, too. In this story, Alex was nervous and needed to find out about his dad's surprise. In the end, it's a great surprise because Alex always wanted to visit California. With that knowledge, he would be able to easily complete his homework assignment that the reader learned about in the first paragraph. The author did a great job of revisiting the beginning and writing a circular ending.

Take a look back at the story you wrote and use the checklist below to help you evaluate your own writing.

- How did you start your story? I started with my character . . .

  _____ thinking

  _____ talking

  _____ involved in an action

  _____ or I wrote a descriptive scene

- How about the middle of your story?

  _____ I had good word choice

  _____ I used show, don't tell details

- How did you end the story?

  _____ I solved my problem

- I ended with my character . . .

  _____ thinking

  _____ talking

  _____ involved in an action

  _____ or I created a circular ending

CHAPTER 5

EXPLANATORY WRITING (p. 134)

"Time for the yard sale!" my mom called from the garage. "Everyone pick things from your room that you don't want anymore." What would I sell? If I looked around my room, I might sell some action figures, old board games, or some books I do not read anymore. One thing I would never sell is my baseball glove.

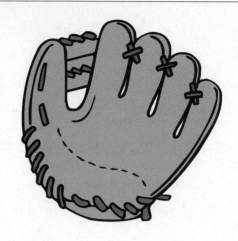

I have the best baseball glove in the whole world. It is soft and broken in perfectly. I have been using it for the last four years. Parting with this glove would be impossible because my grandfather, Pop Pop, gave it to me for my sixth birthday. It was my favorite gift that day and is still my favorite thing.

When I play baseball with my glove, I think I play a little better because of it. Since I have had it for four years, it is perfectly broken in. The ball fits perfectly in the webbing, and I never miss when the ball is hit to me. I always pretend I am in the World Series and playing for my favorite team.

My baseball glove is very special to me. My grandfather gave it to me on my sixth birthday. It was the last gift my grandfather gave me before he passed away. Looking at my glove, I feel a little closer to him. The day the glove doesn't fit my hand anymore will make me very sad. Even if it does not fit, I will never get rid of my glove.

Everyone has something that is important to them. My important item is my baseball glove. I could never part with it, especially at a yard

sale. It is my good luck charm, has sentimental value, and is my favorite thing in the whole world.

Explanation

This response fully explains what item the author would not sell at the family yard sale. The author has a very warm tone to the entire composition and shows the reader how much he loves his baseball glove. Tying the glove's importance to his love for his grandfather makes the story more authentic and shows a mature writing style for a fifth grade student. This composition would receive a 5 on the rubric.

How did you do? What did you choose to write about? Check your writing with the rubric to see what you think your essay would receive as a score. Are there any areas you could improve? What did you do well? Keep up the good work. You will have more chances to write in the practice tests.

CHAPTER 6

WRITING COMPLETE SENTENCES (pp. 140–141)

1. This is only a subject. The sentence is about a lonely boy, but what did the lonely boy do? You needed to provide the answer by writing a predicate or action for the sentence.

   Possible answers: The lonely boy tried to make new friends.

   The lonely boy joined the basketball team.

   The lonely boy missed his best friend.

2. This sentence consists of only a subject. The sentence is about an angry teacher, but what did the angry teacher do? You need to provide the action or predicate for the sentence.

   Possible answers: The angry teacher gave the students detention.

   The angry teacher yelled at the class.

   The angry teacher stomped her foot.

3. This sentence has the action but doesn't tell the reader who is doing the action. Who is playing video games for hours? You need to provide the answer by writing the subject.

   Possible answers: Jordan and Paul played video games for hours.

   The competitive sisters played video games for hours.

4. This sentence includes only the action but not the subject. Who is announcing he won the lottery.

    Possible answers: My cousin announced he won the lottery.

    Mr. Turner, my neighbor, announced he won the lottery.

SENTENCE STRUCTURE (pp. 143–144)

Comma Splices and Run-on Sentences

1. Tyler dove for the ball, and he made the third out.

    Tyler dove for the ball. He made the third out.

    Since Tyler dove for the ball, he made the third out.

2. Josie performed in the talent show. She won first place.

    Josie performed in the talent show, and she won first place.

    When Josie performed in the talent show, she won first place.

3. My cat cuddled on the couch, and he purred when I pet him.

    My cat cuddled on the couch. He purred when I pet him.

    Cuddling on the couch, my cat purred when I pet him.

4. Reed studied for her science test. She aced it.

    Reed studied for her science test, and she aced it.

    After Reed studied for her science test, she aced it.

SENTENCE VARIETY (p. 145)

1. This sentence needs to include a subject and predicate.

   Possible answers: I love to read thriller books.

   I play soccer in the fall.

2. Each compound sentence consists of two independent clauses. Both could stand alone as a complete sentence.

   Possible answers: I love to read thriller books, and then I write thriller stories.

   I play soccer in the fall, and I play baseball in the spring.

3. Writing an independent clause with one or more dependent clauses forms a complex sentence.

   Possible answers: In addition to reading thriller books, I write them.

   After playing baseball in the spring, I play soccer in the fall.

HOMOPHONES (pp. 148–149)

1. The brothers spent hours playing <u>their</u> video games. (The video games belong to the brothers; therefore, the correct answer is "their.")

2. Molly ordered a <u>plain</u> donut rather than one with sprinkles.

3. Jaime looked <u>through</u> his binder for the homework.

4. I don't know <u>whether</u> I should go for a run or a hike.

5. The <u>effect</u> of the fire was devastating.

6. Melissa has <u>too</u> many pairs of shoes.

7. My parents <u>affect</u> the decisions I make.

8. The teacher asked Michele to read the paragraph <u>aloud</u>.

9. Listen closely and you will <u>hear</u> the sounds of crickets.

10. I like math better <u>than</u> science.

DIALOGUE (p. 151)

1. "Who handed in their permission slips?" Mrs. Jones asked.

2. Nick said, "I'll be in my room if you need me."

3. "On Tuesday you can come bowling," said Samantha. "If you like soccer, you should come to the park on Saturday."

4. "Today we will practice passing and dribbling," Coach Magnotti said.

5. "We will begin the experiment by gathering our materials, Ms. Kaufhold directed, "and then we will dissect the worm."

DIALOGUE (p. 153)

"Come on Leo. No one's going to find out," Harley said as he paced across the room.

"I don't know," Leo replied softly with his dark eyes staring down at his clasped hands.

"I'm sure Ryan will let me copy. He's a good friend," Harley snapped.

"It's just that I studied really hard and I don't want to lose points if we get caught," Leo replied. He didn't want to see Harley fail but he didn't want to cheat either.

"Trust me, we won't get caught," Harley pleaded in a desperate voice. This was his only chance of passing Math. Why hadn't he studied like Leo?

"Maybe you should ask Ryan," Leo said. He knew it was the right thing to do yet he found it hard to look at Harley. If Harley was a real friend, he never would have asked him to cheat in the first place.

I AND ME (pp. 155–156)

1. Mia, Hannah, Rhea and <u>I</u> will be a group for the project.

2. Toby and <u>I</u> went to the library to study for the science exam.

3. Would you like to hang out with Sam, Nicole, and <u>me</u>?

4. Please, come to the dance with Dan and <u>me</u>.

5. Michele hit Grace and <u>me</u> home with her triple.

PRACTICE TESTS

Congratulations! You have completed the instructional chapters on how to prepare for the NJ ASK 5. Now, you will have the opportunity to put all of this knowledge to use as you take two practice tests. Make sure you read the directions in each section, and pay close attention to the time limits. Good luck! When you are finished, check your answers at the back of the book.

ANSWER SHEET
PRACTICE TEST 1

Part 1
Reading Task

1. Ⓐ Ⓑ Ⓒ Ⓓ   5. Ⓐ Ⓑ Ⓒ Ⓓ   9. Ⓐ Ⓑ Ⓒ Ⓓ

2. Ⓐ Ⓑ Ⓒ Ⓓ   6. Ⓐ Ⓑ Ⓒ Ⓓ   10. Ⓐ Ⓑ Ⓒ Ⓓ

3. Ⓐ Ⓑ Ⓒ Ⓓ   7. Ⓐ Ⓑ Ⓒ Ⓓ   11. Use answer space in test.

4. Ⓐ Ⓑ Ⓒ Ⓓ   8. Ⓐ Ⓑ Ⓒ Ⓓ

Part 2
Writing Task

Use answer space in test.

Part 3
Reading Task

1. Ⓐ Ⓑ Ⓒ Ⓓ   5. Ⓐ Ⓑ Ⓒ Ⓓ   9. Ⓐ Ⓑ Ⓒ Ⓓ

2. Ⓐ Ⓑ Ⓒ Ⓓ   6. Ⓐ Ⓑ Ⓒ Ⓓ   10. Ⓐ Ⓑ Ⓒ Ⓓ

3. Ⓐ Ⓑ Ⓒ Ⓓ   7. Ⓐ Ⓑ Ⓒ Ⓓ   11. Use answer space in test.

4. Ⓐ Ⓑ Ⓒ Ⓓ   8. Ⓐ Ⓑ Ⓒ Ⓓ

Part 4

Writing Task

Use answer space in test.

PRACTICE TEST 1

PART 1—READING TASK

Directions: Read the story of *Black Beauty's Breaking In* and then answer the questions that follow. You will have 30 minutes to complete the task.

Breaking In
(Excerpt from *Black Beauty* by Anna Sewell)

I was now beginning to grow handsome; my coat had grown fine and soft, and was bright black. I had one white foot and a pretty white star on my forehead. I was thought very handsome; my master would not sell me till I was four years old; he said lads ought not to work like men, and colts ought not to work like horses till they were quite grown up.

When I was four years old Squire Gordon came to look at me. He examined my eyes, my mouth, and my legs; he felt them all down; and then I had to walk and trot and gallop before him. He seemed to like me, and said, "When he has been well broken in he will do very well." My master said he would break me in himself, as he should not like me to be frightened or hurt, and he lost no time about it, for the next day he began.

Every one may not know what breaking in is, therefore I will describe it. It means to teach a horse to wear a saddle and bridle, and to carry on his back a man, woman or child; to go just the way they wish, and to go quietly. Besides this he has to learn to

---

wear a collar, a crupper, and a breeching, and to stand still while they are put on; then to have a cart or a chaise fixed behind, so that he cannot walk or trot without dragging it after him; and he must go fast or slow, just as his driver wishes. He must never start at what he sees, nor speak to other horses, nor bite, nor kick, nor have any will of his own; but always do his master's will, even though he may be very tired or hungry; but the worst of all is, when his harness is once on, he may neither jump for joy nor lie down for weariness. So you see this breaking in is a great thing.

I had of course long been used to a halter and a headstall, and to be led about in the fields and lanes quietly, but now I was to have a bit and bridle; *my master gave me some oats as usual, and after a good deal of coaxing he got the bit into my mouth, and the bridle fixed, but it was a nasty thing!* Those who have never had a bit in their mouths cannot think how bad it feels; a great piece of cold hard steel as thick as a man's finger to be pushed into one's mouth, between one's teeth, and over one's tongue, with the ends coming out at the corner of your mouth, and held fast there by straps over your head, under your throat, round your nose, and under your chin; so that no way in the world can you get rid of the nasty hard thing; it is very bad! Yes, very bad! At least I thought so; but I knew my mother always wore one when she went out, and all horses did when they were grown up; and so, what with the nice oats, and what with my master's pats, kind words, and gentle ways, I got to wear my bit and bridle.

Next came the saddle, but that was not half so bad; my master put it on my back very gently, while old Daniel held my head; he then made the girths fast under my body, patting and talking to me all the time; then I had a few oats, then a little leading about; and this he did every day till I began to look for the oats and the saddle. At length, one morning, my master got on my back and rode me round the meadow on the soft grass. It certainly did feel queer; but I must say I felt rather proud to carry my master, and as he continued to ride me a little every day I soon became accustomed to it.

The next unpleasant business was putting on the iron shoes; that too was very hard at first. My master went with me to the smith's forge, to see that I was not hurt or got any fright. The blacksmith took my feet in his hand, one after the other, and cut away some of the hoof. It did not pain me, so I stood still on three legs till he had done them all. Then he took a piece of iron the shape of my foot, and clapped it on, and drove some nails through the shoe quite into my hoof, so that the shoe was firmly on. My feet felt very stiff and heavy, but in time I got used to it.

1. The narrator of the story is _____.

   A. the master

   B. a young girl

   C. a young boy

   D. a horse

2. Why does Squire Gordon examine the narrator's eyes, mouth, and legs?

   A. He is a doctor.

   B. He wants to buy Black Beauty.

   C. He is the master.

   D. He is the trainer for Black Beauty.

3. How does the reader know the master truly cares for Black Beauty?

   A. The master said he would break Black Beauty in himself, as he should not like him to be frightened or hurt.

   B. The master went with Black Beauty to the blacksmith for shoes.

   C. The master bought new clothes for Black Beauty.

   D. Both A and B

4. Breaking in teaches a horse to _____.

   A. wear a saddle and bridle

   B. carry a man, woman, or child

   C. pull a cart or chaise

   D. all of the above

5. The narrator views wearing a _____ as a symbol of adulthood because his mother and other adults wear it.

   A. suit

   B. saddle

   C. bit

   D. rein

6. In paragraph four, the narrator says, "My master gave me some oats as usual, and after a good deal of <u>coaxing</u> he got the bit into my mouth, and the bridle fixed, but it was a nasty thing!" Define coaxing.

   A. To persuade

   B. To feed

   C. To brush

   D. To anger

7. How did the master get Black Beauty to wear the bit?

   A. He forced him.

   B. He fed him nice oats and had kind words.

   C. He paid him.

   D. Both A and B

8. How did Black Beauty feel when he carried the master?

   A. Tired

   B. Proud

   C. Angry

   D. All of the above

9. How are Black Beauty's shoes different than the shoes you wear today?

   A. They are iron and held on with nails.

   B. They are silver and held on with nails.

   C. They are leather like shoes today.

   D. They are black and shiny.

10. What will happen to Black Beauty now that he has his shoes?

    A. He will run a race.

    B. He will see his mother.

    C. He will eat oats.

    D. He will go live with Squire Gordon.

11. The process of being broken in is necessary but
difficult. Do you think it is fair for the narrator to be
put through this process? Use evidence from the text
to support your answer.

_____

_____

_____

_____

_____

_____

_____

_____

_____

_____

_____

_____

_____

_____

PART 2—WRITING TASK—PERSUASIVE PROMPT

Your school is going to invite someone famous to speak at your school. Your principal has asked for suggestions as to who should be invited. Write a letter to your principal stating who you think the school should invite. Make sure to use clear reasons to support your choice.

You may use the space below to prewrite. Write your essay on the four lined pages that follow. You have 45 minutes for this part of the test.

PART 2—WRITING TEST—PERSUASIVE PROMPT

PART 3—READING TASK

Directions: You will have 30 minutes to read the passage and answer the questions.

Snow Day Adventures

Every kid wishes and hopes for that cold, winter morning when Mom or Dad opens the door to the bedroom and whispers, "No school today." Immediately, the corners of the mouth curve upward and the covers are tugged a little tighter for a few more hours of sleep. There is nothing better than a much needed snow day. However, there may be some who don't know how to <u>adequately</u> use a day off and simply waste it away playing video games. There are many interesting ways to spend a snow day.

The most obvious way to spend this time is to go outside to play. Not only is it fun, but playing in the snow also provides great exercise. A person's first instinct might be to say, "It's cold outside!" Well, don't let that stop you! Just bundle up and have a good time. Make sure to layer clothing and wear a warm hat, gloves, and a pair of boots. The next question may be, "What do I do once I'm outside?" The possibilities are endless.

The snow can be used for a good old-fashioned snowball fight, a snowman or a snow fort, sledding, and snow angels. Many kids have experience building a snowman or sledding, but some have never faced the challenge of building a snow fort. First, decide what kind of fort to make. An igloo, a tunnel, or a cave are all building possibilities. First, find a snowdrift or make a big pile of snow. If the snow doesn't feel like it is strong enough to dig into, try pouring cold water over the top to make a layer of ice. Once the pile of snow is ready, start digging. Dig completely through to make a tunnel or just hollow the inside out to make an igloo. A wider opening will make the fort feel like a cave. The more creative the plan, the more fun this adventure will be. Try making snow furniture or snow sculptures or this new snow home.

Instead of spending time outside, spend the snow day playing games with family or friends in the neighborhood. Now, this doesn't mean turn on the X-box. Instead, take out some of the board games sitting on the top shelf of the closet. Perhaps a game of Clue, Monopoly, Sorry, or cards will pass the time. Playing games provides quality time to socialize. Most importantly, a board game will never be played the same way, so it is fun and spontaneous.

There is something about a snow day that makes people want to bake or cook a tasty treat. Of course, this should always be done with adult supervision. Warm chocolate chip cookies, homemade pizza, or a simple cup of hot chocolate are all scrumptious possibilities. For a twist, try experimenting with new pizza toppings. Put interesting veggies like eggplant on top, or try a unique topping like shrimp. Again, spending time with Mom or Dad in the kitchen will create lasting memories and may lead to the discovery of a new favorite food.

Furthermore, crafts would be an additional way to spend the day. Perhaps building a scrapbook would be a creative and practical project. On the other hand, this would also be an <u>ideal</u> day for trying a new craft. For example, making a tie-dye shirt, decorating a picture frame, or making a sock puppet could pass the hours. In addition to making puppets, a show could be performed.

Finally, curling up with a good book or writing in a journal are popular options for snow days. This is a fantastic choice for those looking to sit and relax. Often, it is difficult to find time for these activities and a snow day is the perfect opportunity.

Any of these choices would be an incredible way to spend a day home from school. Whether outside in the fresh air or staying warm in the comfort of a home, any of these activities will certainly create an enjoyable and memorable day.

1. In paragraph one, the author states, "However, there may be some who don't know how to <u>adequately</u> use a day off and simply waste it away playing video games." Define adequately.

   A. Appropriately

   B. Happily

   C. Quietly

   D. Warmly

2. What is the main idea of the article?

   A. Kids should play outside on a snow day.

   B. Playing video games is a great way to spend a snow day.

   C. Building a fort is fun.

   D. There are many activities to keep kids busy on a snow day.

3. What does the author suggest as outside activities?

   A. Build a snowman.

   B. Make a snow fort.

   C. Have a snowball fight.

   D. All of the above

4. Which is NOT a step in making a snow fort?

   A. Find or make a snowdrift.

   B. Pour cold water over the snow to make a thin layer of ice.

   C. Pull a sled over the drift.

   D. Dig out a hole to crawl through.

5. Why is a game a great way to spend a snow day?

    A. It gives you an opportunity to socialize with friends and family.

    B. It can make you rich.

    C. Every game is new and unique.

    D. Both A and C

6. The author suggested each of the following baking or cooking ideas except _____.

    A. tacos

    B. pizza

    C. cookies

    D. hot chocolate

7. According to the article, how could pizza become more interesting?

    A. Order from the pizza parlor.

    B. Experiment with new toppings.

    C. Try making upside-down pizza.

    D. Make a stromboli instead.

8. In paragraph six, the author states, "On the other hand, this would also be an ideal day for trying a new craft." What does ideal mean?

    A. Boring

    B. Cold

    C. Perfect

    D. Worst

9. The author suggests all of the following crafts except
   _____.

   A. painting

   B. scrap booking

   C. tie dying

   D. sock puppets

10. The author suggests _____ as an alternative
    to reading.

    A. playing video games

    B. drawing

    C. singing

    D. writing

11. The article offers many suggestions for snow day
entertainment. Which idea do you think would be
the best way to spend your snow day? Use evidence
from text to support your answer.

_____

_____

_____

_____

_____

_____

_____

_____

_____

_____

_____

_____

_____

PART 4—WRITING TASK—EXPLANATORY PROMPT

Your class has been asked to complete a survey about school. One question asks, "What is your favorite subject in school?" Write a composition that explains what your favorite school subject is. Be sure to give examples explaining why it is your favorite subject. You have 30 minutes to complete this task.

You may use the space below to do your prewriting.

ANSWER SHEET
PRACTICE TEST 2

Part 1

Reading Task

1. Ⓐ Ⓑ Ⓒ Ⓓ   5. Ⓐ Ⓑ Ⓒ Ⓓ   9. Ⓐ Ⓑ Ⓒ Ⓓ

2. Ⓐ Ⓑ Ⓒ Ⓓ   6. Ⓐ Ⓑ Ⓒ Ⓓ   10. Ⓐ Ⓑ Ⓒ Ⓓ

3. Ⓐ Ⓑ Ⓒ Ⓓ   7. Ⓐ Ⓑ Ⓒ Ⓓ   11. Use answer space in test.

4. Ⓐ Ⓑ Ⓒ Ⓓ   8. Ⓐ Ⓑ Ⓒ Ⓓ

Part 2

Writing Task

Use answer space in test.

Part 3

Reading Task

1. Ⓐ Ⓑ Ⓒ Ⓓ   5. Ⓐ Ⓑ Ⓒ Ⓓ   9. Ⓐ Ⓑ Ⓒ Ⓓ

2. Ⓐ Ⓑ Ⓒ Ⓓ   6. Ⓐ Ⓑ Ⓒ Ⓓ   10. Ⓐ Ⓑ Ⓒ Ⓓ

3. Ⓐ Ⓑ Ⓒ Ⓓ   7. Ⓐ Ⓑ Ⓒ Ⓓ   11. Use answer space in test.

4. Ⓐ Ⓑ Ⓒ Ⓓ   8. Ⓐ Ⓑ Ⓒ Ⓓ

Part 4

Writing Task

Use answer space in test.

PRACTICE TEST 2

PART 1—READING TASK

Directions: Read the story of Mary and then answer the
questions that follow. You will have 30 minutes to
complete the task.

Mary, Mary, Quite Contrary
(From *The Secret Garden* by Frances Hodgson Burnett)

Mary had liked to look at her mother from a distance and she
had thought her very pretty, but as she knew very little of her
she could scarcely have been expected to love her or to miss her
very much when she was gone. She did not miss her at all, in
fact, and as she was a <u>self-absorbed</u> child she gave her entire
thought to herself, as she had always done. If she had been older
she would no doubt have been very anxious at being left alone in
the world, but she was very young, and as she had always been
taken care of, she supposed she always would be. What she
thought was that she would like to know if she was going to nice
people, who would be polite to her and give her her own way as
her Ayah and the other native servants had done.

She knew that she was not going to stay at the English
clergyman's house where she was taken at first. She did not want
to stay. The English clergyman was poor and he had five
children nearly all the same age and they wore shabby clothes
and were always quarreling and snatching toys from each other.
Mary hated their untidy bungalow and was so disagreeable to

---

them that after the first day or two nobody would play with her. By the second day they had given her a nickname which made her furious.

It was Basil who thought of it first. Basil was a little boy with impudent blue eyes and a turned-up nose, and Mary hated him. She was playing by herself under a tree, just as she had been playing the day the cholera broke out. She was making heaps of earth and paths for a garden and Basil came and stood near to watch her. Presently he got rather interested and suddenly made a suggestion.

"Why don't you put a heap of stones there and pretend it is a rockery?" he said. "There in the middle," and he leaned over her to point.

"Go away!" cried Mary. "I don't want boys. Go away!" For a moment Basil looked angry, and then he began to tease. He was always teasing his sisters. He danced round and round her and made faces and sang and laughed.

> "Mistress Mary, quite contrary,
> How does your garden grow?
> With silver bells, and cockle shells,
> And marigolds all in a row."

He sang it until the other children heard and laughed, too; and the crosser Mary got, the more they sang "Mistress Mary, quite contrary"; and after that as long as she stayed with them they called her "Mistress Mary Quite Contrary" when they spoke of her to each other, and often when they spoke to her.

"You are going to be sent home," Basil said to her, "at the end of the week. And we're glad of it."

"I am glad of it, too," answered Mary. "Where is home?"

"She doesn't know where home is!" said Basil, with seven-year-old scorn. "It's England, of course. Our grandmama lives there and our sister Mabel was sent to her last year. You are not going to your grandmama. You have none. You are going to your uncle. His name is Mr. Archibald Craven."

"I don't know anything about him," snapped Mary.

"I know you don't," Basil answered. "You don't know anything. Girls never do. I heard father and mother talking about him. He lives in a great, big, <u>desolate</u> old house in the country and no one goes near him. He's so cross he won't let them, and they wouldn't come if he would let them. He's a hunchback, and he's horrid." "I don't believe you," said Mary; and she turned her back and stuck her fingers in her ears, because she would not listen any more.

But she thought over it a great deal afterward; and when Mrs. Crawford told her that night that she was going to sail away to England in a few days and go to her uncle, Mr. Archibald Craven, who lived at Misselthwaite Manor, she looked so stony and stubbornly uninterested that they did not know what to think about her. They tried to be kind to her, but she only turned her face away when Mrs. Crawford attempted to kiss her, and held herself stiffly when Mr. Crawford patted her shoulder.

"She is such a plain child," Mrs. Crawford said pityingly, afterward. "And her mother was such a pretty creature. She had a very pretty manner, too, and Mary has the most unattractive ways I ever saw in a child. The children call her 'Mistress Mary Quite Contrary,' and though it's naughty of them, one can't help understanding it."

1. What happened to Mary's mother?

   A. She is on vacation.

   B. She is working.

   C. She died.

   D. None of the above

2. In paragraph one, Mary is described as self-absorbed. This means she _____.

   A. is selfish

   B. makes friends easily

   C. is unhappy

   D. Both A and C

3. Why didn't Mary want to stay at the English clergyman's house?

   A. The bungalow was untidy.

   B. The kids quarreled.

   C. The family was poor.

   D. All of the above

4. What nickname did the kids give Mary?

   A. Mary had a little lamb

   B. Mistress Mary quite contrary

   C. Mean Mistress Mary

   D. Mistress Mary always scary

5. Why did they call her this nickname?

   A. Mary likes to scare the kids.

   B. Mary is difficult and doesn't get along with others.

   C. Mary likes to rhyme.

   D. Mary likes animals.

6. Where will Mary go after the clergyman's house?

   A. To her uncle's house in England

   B. To her uncle's house in France

   C. To her Aunt's house in England

   D. To her Aunt's house in France

7. Archibald Craven's house is described as "a great, big, <u>desolate</u> old house in the country." What does *desolate* mean?

   A. Lovely

   B. Scary

   C. Huge

   D. Dreary

8. Basil described Archibald Craven as all of the following except _____.

   A. cross

   B. hunchback

   C. horrid

   D. greedy

9. How is Mary different than her mother?

   A. She is plain.

   B. She does not have good manners.

   C. She is beautiful.

   D. Both A and B

10. What is Mrs. Crawford's opinion of Mary?

    A. She thinks Mary is like her mother.

    B. She loves Mary like a daughter.

    C. She doesn't like Mary.

    D. She thinks Mary is a funny child.

11. Would you rather be friends with Mary or Basil? Use evidence from the text to support your answer.

_____

_____

_____

_____

_____

_____

_____

_____

_____

_____

_____

_____

_____

_____

_____

_____

_____

_____

PART 2—WRITING TASK—SPECULATIVE PROMPT

When you walk into class, your teacher asks you to see her after class. She mentions that you are not in trouble, but she needs to tell you something. Write a story about what your teacher tells you and how it makes you feel.

You have 30 minutes for this part of the test. Use the space below to prewrite.

PART 3—READING TASK

Directions: You will have 30 minutes to read the passage and answer the questions.

How to Find a Good Book

Finding a good book can be a challenge for many people. Sometimes it is hard to figure out exactly what you want to read. You may choose a book that looks good and then realize it is too difficult or doesn't hold your interest. Before you give up, remember, with the right strategies you can find the perfect book.

One place you can begin your search is the local bookstore. Often, people who work in the store have a <u>vast</u> knowledge of books and can help you find something based on your interests. Spend time browsing the shelves and reading the back cover or book jacket for information about the book. The synopsis of the book will help you decide if it is worth a shot. You might even discover useful reviews or a list of awards. Furthermore, look for a recommended reading list. Here you will find books recommended by employees of the store and possibly something that peeks your interest.

In addition, talk to friends and family about books they have read. Usually your friends share similar interests. Therefore, if they enjoyed a book, there is good chance you'll enjoy it, too. It might surprise you to learn that your parents have a favorite book from when they were your age. Take a chance and ask your Mom, Dad, or any family member to make a recommendation. Not only will you discover a good book, but also you'll have fun discussing the story with your friends or family.

Reading reviews is another fantastic way to find great books. Book reviews can be found in the newspaper, on the internet, or in your favorite magazine. Sometimes magazines will even provide you with an excerpt of the book. This really gives you the opportunity to see if you will like the author's style and the content of the book. You could even take this strategy with you when browsing books. Instead of just looking at the cover, take a few minutes to read the first few pages of the book. This allows you to determine if the book is interesting and understandable.

When you find an author you like, stick with him or her. Often, an author has published several books; if you discover you like a story, see if there are others. When you do find an author you like, write their name down. A list of favorite books and authors will make it easier when searching for a new book to read. You could also make a list of books you want to read so you don't forget. If you see an interesting title in the bookstore or a friend mentions a good read, write it down for another time. Look around at what other people are reading and if it looks interesting, add it to the list. If you use this method, you'll always have something to pick up next and won't be left desperately searching for a book you will like.

Finally, you have an incredible resource closer than you think. Find time to talk to the school or public librarian. Many times, the librarian can help you find new authors who are similar to your favorites. In addition, they may give you strategies for checking if a book is too difficult for you. Some librarians teach the five-finger rule. In order to use this strategy, flip the book open to a full-length page in the middle of the book. Start reading the text, and each time you find a word you don't know, put one finger up. If you find you have five fingers up, then the book is too hard, and you should add it to your list to read when you are a little older. If you don't have any fingers up, it may be too easy, but use your judgment, and if it is something you really want to read, go for it.

Finding a good book is not always easy, but it is worth the search. Just remember, sometimes you need to give a book a chance. Some of the best books may start off a little slow, but if you hang in there, it could turn into a favorite. Always keep your eyes and ears open for good books, and you'll never be left wondering what to read next.

1. Why can it be difficult to find a good book to read?

   A. You don't know what you want to read.

   B. A book is too difficult.

   C. A book doesn't hold your interest.

   D. All of the above

2. What is the main idea of the article?

   A. Ask friends to recommend books.

   B. If you use strategies, you can find a good book.

   C. Keep lists of what you want to read.

   D. Reading is important.

3. In paragraph two, the author states, "Often, people who work in the store have a <u>vast</u> knowledge of books and can help you find something based on your interests." Define *vast*.

   A. Interesting

   B. Small amount

   C. Huge amount

   D. None of the above

4. Why is it easy to find a great book at the bookstore?

   A. The people who work there know a lot about books.

   B. They often have employee recommendations.

   C. You can spend time browsing lots of books and reading the back covers.

   D. All of the above

5. Why might friends be a good source of finding books?

    A. Usually friends share similar interests.

    B. Your friends might work at a bookstore.

    C. Friends always know what is on the bestseller list.

    D. Friends can tell you which movies were books first.

6. According to the author, what might be surprising when you talk to your parents about books?

    A. They don't know any good books.

    B. They can recommend favorite books from when they were your age.

    C. They like to read.

    D. They know a famous author.

7. How do you know if a book will be too hard for you to read?

    A. It tells you on the back of the book.

    B. Your friend tells you it is too hard.

    C. You do the five-finger test.

    D. You won't know if it is too hard.

8. Which of the following is NOT part of the five-finger test?

   A. Open the book to any full-length page in the book.

   B. Begin reading and put one finger up for each word you don't know.

   C. Use your finger to read the back cover and decide if the book is too hard.

   D. Check how many fingers you have up to determine if the book is too hard.

9. According to the author, why should you keep a list of books?

   A. You will always know what to read next.

   B. You won't forget a book that you heard about from a friend or family member.

   C. You can publish your list.

   D. Both A and B

10. The article suggests, if a book doesn't catch your interest right away, you should _____.

   A. close the book immediately

   B. Read a little further to give it a chance.

   C. Return the book to the library or bookstore.

   D. Tell people to never read the book.

11. There are many strategies to use when looking for a good book. Which strategy do you think works the best? Explain why using evidence from the text.

_____

_____

_____

_____

_____

_____

_____

_____

_____

_____

_____

_____

_____

_____

PART 4—WRITING TASK—EXPLANATORY PROMPT

Students, first read the poem "Things That Go Bump in the Night!" then read the prompt that follows.

My heart beats faster as I reach to turn off the light
Will tonight be better or still filled with fright?
The darkness surrounds me and sits on my chest
Am I alone in my fear or another among the rest?
How do I end it and make it do away?
Can I get rid of it or is it destined to stay?
I look under the bed and behind the closet door
Nothing to fear there and I calm a little more.
Fear cannot stop me from relaxing in my bed
I lay on my pillow and close my eyes with nothing more to
    dread.

Has there ever been something that you feared? Write about your fear. Make sure you include the following:
What did you fear and why did you fear it?
Did your fear stop you from being able to do something?
Explain how you overcame your fear or what you can do to overcome it.

You have 30 minutes for this part of the test. Use the space below to prewrite.

ANSWERS TO PRACTICE TESTS

PRACTICE TEST 1

PART 1—READING TASK

1. **D.** Clues that the narrator is a horse include being called a colt, galloping, wearing a saddle and bridle.

2. **B.** The reader must draw this conclusion because Squire Gordon is examining him and states that he will do well once he is broken in.

3. **B.** Master doesn't want anything bad to happen to Black Beauty so he breaks him in himself and goes with him to the blacksmith. He is protective of Black Beauty throughout the story.

4. **D.** Breaking in teaches a horse to wear a saddle and bridle, carry a person, and pull a cart or chaise.

5. **C.** The author states this in paragraph four.

6. **A.** The reader knows this because the master had to give Black Beauty oats to bribe him to take the bit in his mouth.

7. **B.** Black Beauty took the bit when the owner fed him oats and had kind words.

8. **B.** Black Beauty felt proud when he carried the master.

9. **A.** They are iron and held on with nails.

10. **D.** He will go live with Squire Gordon. The reader knows this because after Squire Gordon examined Black Beauty he said, "When he has been well broken in he will do very well." This indicates that he will buy Black Beauty.

11. Check your own answer to see if you included each of the following parts. Then, read the sample answer below.

_____ I restated the question?

_____ I used evidence from the text?

_____ I made a personal connection?

_____ I have a concluding sentence?

I think that it is fair for a horse to go through the process of being broken in. Sooner or later, most horses go through this process, so it's better to get it over with at a younger age. When this book was written, horses were mainly used for transportation of people and goods and, of course, for the pleasure of riding. For all of these things, a trained horse is needed. A horse needs to know how to wear a saddle and a bridle, carry weight on its back, and pull a cart. If horses weren't broken in, they would not be able to help people at all.

PART 2—WRITING TASK

Sample Persuasive Writing Response

More than half of the fifth grade students in the state of New Jersey cannot identify the current Governor of New Jersey. It is facts like this that make it necessary for our school to ask the governor to come speak at our school. Our school is going to invite one person to come speak at our school, and our school should ask the governor to speak because we could ask questions about our school, learn about his job, and meet the most important man in our state.

First of all, if the governor was invited to our school, we could ask important questions about our school. Even though we are young, students our age worry about our school and whether or not we will keep things we think are important. We worry about keeping physical education and recess. They might not be important to parents or other adults, but we need to make sure the government has enough money to keep programs like art, music, and gym. If the governor came to talk to us, we could ask our own questions.

Second of all, we could ask the governor questions about government. We are young, but we have a lot of questions. Since we are getting older, we can ask questions about how our government works. Most students do not know the difference between the government of the state of New Jersey and the government in Washington, D.C. The governor could explain all of these things to us. We would understand how government in the state of New Jersey works and how it affects people our age every day.

Finally, the governor is the most important and powerful person in New Jersey. That would be a fabulous honor for our school. If the governor came to our school, newspapers would come to our school, and maybe some students could be interviewed by the newspaper. The governor is in charge of the whole state. By coming to our school, it would show how important he thinks our school is. Everybody would be so excited.

In conclusion, the only choice for our school is the governor of New Jersey. He would answer questions we have and teach us about government. He is also the most important person in New Jersey. There may be other people who could teach the students of our school something, but none of them are as important as the governor. Our school and its students would never forget having the opportunity to listen to the governor talk and show us how much he cares about people our age. He is the only choice.

Explanation

This essay is an excellent example of a persuasive essay. The student was instructed to write an essay to the principal about whom he or she would invite to come to their school and speak. It was well planned, used strong vocabulary for a student in fifth grade, and has very few, if any, mistakes. This essay would earn a 5 as a score.

Using the rubric, compare your essay and the essay in this book. Did you prewrite before you wrote your essay? Did you use all of the techniques discussed in the persuasive essay chapter? What score would you give your essay? Reread the example essay. The author was clear in his or her choice of speaker. He or she gave three clear reasons why the governor should be chosen by the principal.

Look through your essay. Are there any areas you missed? How could you fix it next time?

PART 3—READING TASK

1. **A.** If someone is not using the day "adequately," that person is wasting it. If a person is using it adequately, he or she must be doing something worthwhile. Therefore, adequate means suitable or appropriate.

2. **D.** This is the correct answer because the article is about many different activities, not just one.

3. **D.** The author suggests building a snowman, making a fort, or having a snowball fight.

4. **C.** Pulling a sled over the drift is not a step in building a snow fort.

5. **D.** Playing a game gives you an opportunity to socialize with friends and family and is different every time you play, which makes it new and unique.

6. **A.** The author suggests making pizza, cookies, or hot chocolate.

7. **B.** The author suggests using interesting vegetables like eggplant or unique ingredients such as shrimp.

8. **C.** The author is encouraging the reader to try new crafts. Therefore, "perfect" is the best choice.

9. **A.** The author does not mention painting in the article.

10. **D.** The article suggests writing in a journal as an alternative to reading.

11. Check your own answer to see if you included each of the following parts. Then, read the sample answer below.

_____ I restated the question?

_____ I used evidence from the text?

_____ I made a personal connection?

_____ I have a concluding sentence?

> The best way to spend a snow day is to go outside and play. This is the best option because you can get lots of exercise and have fun at the same time. When outside, you could make snow angels, have a snowball fight, or build a fort. When it snows, I usually go outside with my brother and build a snowman. We make the snowman as large as we possibly can and often we are working so hard, we're actually warm instead of cold. No one should waste a good day playing video games when they could be having so much fun outside.

PART 4—WRITING TASK

Sample Explanatory Writing Response

> My fingers softly curve around the pencil, hugging the smooth yellow structure. As I place the pencil onto the paper, I can express myself in every way, even if only with a few simple lines. Writing is my favorite subject. When my

pencil floats across the paper, leaving behind a scatter of letters and thoughts, I become whoever I want to be. There is no limit for my imagination and I can see places that are yet to exist. To me writing is like the glistening stars that shimmer at night. They keep you interested every night and leave you wanting more every day. Out of every subject, writing is my favorite because it lets me express my thoughts, teaches me new things, and it is a new adventure every day.

Sometimes I appear to be lost within my very own thoughts, but when I pick up my pencil and start to write, they slowly spill out. For example, poetry lets me express my feelings in a creative way. It is surprising even when I am following a specific format that my sense of style shows. Freestyle poetry is my favorite type of poem. This is because I can grasp a few thoughts in my head and go whenever I want to go with them. Writing is an original and creative way to let my thoughts come alive.

Learning new techniques in writing is thought provoking, and it grabs my attention. As I start writing class, I learn many new things and then apply them to what I already know. Even techniques taught about persuasive writing draw me in like a fish being reeled to a fisherman. I am never sure where writing will take me. Never did I think that I could enjoy learning so much. I've enjoyed every lesson for every year in writing. Writing is a roller coaster of words, phrases, and techniques that never ends.

The adventures are endless every day in writing class. Peeking into the classroom, a bright light emerges through the small space, pulling me in to a pleasant surprise. I can write my very own stories filled with description in every paragraph. Throughout the rest of my life, writing will be essential.

The sun sets over the serene baby blue water in my own original place. Every word, every phrase, and every story has meaning. Writing sparks something within me that shines all around. Techniques, thoughts, and adventures are all held within writing class.

Explanation

This essay topic instructed the writer to choose his or her favorite subject. The author chose to write about writing class. The composition is well planned and executed. Mature vocabulary is used throughout the essay. The author shows that he or she enjoys writing by using very descriptive language. This writer has a superior command of language and would earn a 5 on this composition.

If you read the composition again, the author obviously planned the essay using a web. The center of the web was writing, and each part of the web was related to the author's enjoyment of writing. By prewriting properly, the author was able to concentrate on adding details and making the essay as good as could be.

PRACTICE TEST 2

PART 1—READING TASK

1. **C.** The reader knows Mary has not been with her mother since she was very little and must draw the conclusion that she has died.

2. **A.** The author states, "She did not miss her at all, in fact, and as she was a self-absorbed child she gave her entire thought to herself, as she had always done." Being selfish means you only think of yourself, so this is the best answer.

3. **D.** The bungalow was untidy, the kids quarreled, and the family was poor.

4. **B.** The author clearly states the kids call Mary Mistress Mary Quite Contrary.

5. **B.** Mary is difficult and doesn't get along with others. *Contrary* means unfavorable and disagreeable which fits her behaviors.

6. **A.** She will be sent to live with Archibald Craven.

7. **D.** *Dreary* is defined as gloomy and sad.

8. **D.** Basil says he is cross, horrid, and hunchback.

9. **D.** Mary is described as plain and ill mannered unlike her mother who was beautiful.

10. **C.** The reader knows she doesn't like Mary because at the end Mrs. Crawford says she understands why the kids call her Mistress Mary quite contrary.

11. Check your own answer to see if you included each of the following parts. Then, read the sample answer below.

_____ I restated the question?

_____ I used evidence from the text?

_____ I made a personal connection?

_____ I have a concluding sentence?

I would rather be a friend to Mary than Basil. Although Mary is a little selfish, Basil is mean and I would rather hang out with someone who is a little selfish than very mean. Maybe Mary is difficult to get along with because she has been alone for so long. I am sure it has not been an easy life without a mother. I can't imagine not having my parents to take care of me and teach me how to get along with others. I think if Mary was around people who were nice and really cared for her, she might change and become more likeable. In the end, I feel sorry for Mary and I would try and become her friend before Basil.

PART 2—WRITING TASK

Sample Speculative Writing Response

Cameron's backpack was a mess as usual. He wondered how all of his papers ended up looking like they had been part of huge paper snowball fight and then shoved back in his bag. He could never remember putting them in like that. It always annoyed Mrs. DeMarco that his homework always looked like that, even though it was always done. Cameron tried to sort through what he would need for class that day and what could wait until tonight to organize. If he didn't get moving he was going to be late.

Rushing into the classroom, Cameron almost knocked down his best friend Kyle.

"Hey, watch it!" Kyle yelled as he jumped out of the way.

"Sorry, all of my homework is a mess again. I wanted to fix it before class started," Cameron said.

"I don't know how you do it, Cam," Kyle chuckled as he entered the room.

Cameron quickly moved between a couple of classmates as he tried to get to his desk and get ready for class. But before he could slide into his seat, he heard the words every student dreads.

"Cameron, could you come up here for a second?" asked Mrs. DeMarco.

Gulp. Cameron was scared to death of those words. He rarely was in trouble, but he always worried about those words. He tried to get up, but his legs weighed about 1,000 pounds. He had to use both arms to push all of his weight out of the chair. He stumbled up to the desk.

"Uh, yes Mrs. DeMarco?" stammered Cameron.

"I just wanted to ask you to stay behind for a minute when everyone goes to gym after class," requested Mrs. DeMarco.

"Okay. Sure. You got it," answered Cameron.

Cameron's legs weighed even more now than before. Had he done something so horrible that Mrs. DeMarco couldn't even speak about it in front of other students? He did not think so. Did his mother call and mention that Cameron was tormenting his little sister at home? No, why would his mother do that? Oh this was going to be torture. Cameron was so upset that he didn't even notice that he walked right past his seat.

"I think you missed something," Kyle said as he snapped Cameron out of his trance.

"Oh. Thanks, Kyle," Cameron whispered.

"Are you okay? You look like you've seen a ghost," Kyle said.

"Mrs. DeMarco needs to see me after class. What could she want? She only does that when kids are really bad," Cameron wondered.

"Good luck, buddy. Glad it's not me!" Kyle laughed.

Cameron slumped into his seat and spent the next 40 minutes thinking of every possible thing he could have done wrong and why Mrs. DeMarco would want to talk to him. Sweat ran down his back, and he felt light-headed. He wondered if he passed out and went to the nurse if Mrs. DeMarco would forget.

Mrs. DeMarco's voice snapped Cameron out of his spell. "Okay, class, I'll see you when you get back from gym. Don't forget we have a math test when you come back."

The class groaned as they walked out. Cameron thought about making a break for it, but his size fives felt like they were locked in cement blocks. He may as well get it over with.

"Mrs. DeMarco, you wanted to see me?" Cameron asked.

"Oh, I almost forgot. Do you remember a few weeks ago when we wrote those poems for the Veteran's Day contest? I received a letter this morning telling me you won first prize! Congratulations! You are going to read your poem to the whole school at the assembly next week. I know you don't like speaking in front of people, so I wanted to tell you first. I didn't want to announce it to the class and make you nervous," Mrs. DeMarco explained.

A contest? Cameron could not believe it. He never thought about anything good. A smile broke out on his face.

"Cameron, do you feel all right? You looked pale during class." Mrs. DeMarco inquired.

"I'm fine. Thanks, Mrs. DeMarco. I just have to remember not to jump to any conclusions," Cameron answered.

Cameron hurried out of class to catch up to Kyle. He could not wait to tell him about this.

Explanation

This story would receive a 5 on the NJ ASK 5. The story uses all of the elements that were discussed in the chapter on speculative writing. The author obviously planned the story very well using the pie chart to prewrite. The story clearly explains what could happen to the student who has to wait to hear about some news from the teacher. The main character's thoughts, actions, and words all relate to the prompt given. The author uses dialogue very well and punctuates it correctly. This story shows a superior command of language for a fifth grader.

Compare the story to your example. Did you complete a prewriting pie chart? Did you have a theme and include it in your story? Did you try to use dialogue and descriptive language. Look at the rubric. What score would you give your story? How can you improve it?

PART 3—READING TASK

1. **D.** The author states all of these as reasons for not finding a good book.

2. **B.** The article is about several different strategies to help the reader accomplish this task. It is not just about asking friends to recommend books, keeping a list, or the importance of reading.

3. **C.** Choice A doesn't make sense because "interesting knowledge" wouldn't help you find a good book. Choice B amount doesn't make sense. If a person works in a bookstore, they should know about books.

4. **D.** Each of these ideas is a strategy that will help you find a good book.

5. **A.** If friends have similar interests, then the books they like may be books you will like.

6. **B.** This is clearly stated in paragraph 3.

7. **C.** If you find there are four or five words on one page that you don't know, you'll probably have a hard time understanding the book. Don't trust the reading level stated on the back of the book. This is not always accurate information.

8. **C.** The other 3 statements are all listed in paragraph 6 as part of the 5-finger rule.

9. **D.** With a list, you always have a book to read next, and you don't forget books you want to read.

10. **B.** Don't immediately give up and close or return a book. You may be surprised that you actually like the book once you get into it.

11. Check your own answer to see if you included each of the following parts. Then, read the sample answer that follows.

_____ I restated the question?

_____ I used evidence from the text?

_____ I made a personal connection?

_____ I have a concluding sentence?

The best strategy for me to use when looking for a good book is to go to the bookstore. At the bookstore I have the opportunity to browse books and look for things I like. Often, the cover is a good indication of whether I will enjoy the book or not. First, I look at the front cover to see if the picture or title grabs my attention. Then, I read the back cover to get an idea of what the story is about. If I really have trouble finding a book, I can ask someone at information to suggest a book about something I enjoy like skateboarding or music, or I can go to the employee recommendation list. Visiting the bookstore is an easy strategy and usually leads to an enjoyable book.

PART 4—WRITING TASK

Sample Explanatory Writing Response

The smell of chlorine filled my nose and almost made me sick to my stomach. I could not go anywhere near a pool because my stomach would be upset and I would be too nervous to move. Going to the beach was difficult also. Hearing the waves crashing against the sand would make my heart race and make me feel like I was going to pass out. All of this was due to my fear of swimming. It seems like a silly fear now, but when I was younger I was terrified.

When I was four years old, I had only been in water a few times. I was not scared yet, but that changed very quickly. I was in a pool at a family party, and my father was holding me in the water. I liked it a lot, and I was splashing the water and having a great time. When I was splashing, I made it hard for my dad to hold on to me. He slipped, and I fell out of his arms. Before I knew it, I was under the water. It was only a second before my father pulled me back up, but the damage was done. From that day on, water petrified me.

Being afraid of the water caused me many problems. I would avoid going anywhere close to water. When friends invited me to pool parties, I would create an excuse so I could not go. One time, a friend invited me to go on vacation with them to the beach. I would have had so much fun, but I did not want to go to the beach. I told my friend that my parents would not let me go. I was too embarrassed to tell my friend I was afraid of the water.

Eventually, my parents talked to me about my fear of the water. They did not want me to grow up and be afraid to go swimming. They suggested that I take lessons and slowly get used to the water. The first time I showed up for swimming lessons, I had to leave. Eventually, I realized that I really liked being in the water. I even started to look forward to going to my lessons. Now, two years later, I even joined a swimming team. Swimming is one of my favorite activities.

Everyone has a fear at one time or another. The important thing is to try to face it. If you face your fear, you might realize that you really had nothing to fear the whole time. That is what happened to me. I almost missed out on an activity that is now my favorite thing to do.

Explanation

This response uses the poem's theme of fear and shows how the author overcame his or her fear of water. The composition showed how the writer first became afraid of water and moved logically toward how he or she overcame the fear. The author used strong vocabulary and varied sentence structure to form a cohesive and interesting essay. The idea of the fear is real, and the author does an excellent job showing how the fear affected his or her life. This prompt would receive a 5 on the NJ ASK.

How did you do? Use the rubric to see how you would score your essay. Did you remember to clearly explain your fear? Did you add enough detail to give the reader a clear picture? Look for ways you can improve your writing the next time you take the test.

INDEX

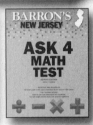

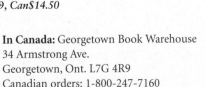

Notes